# A PLACE IN THE SUN

# A PLACE
# IN THE SUN

## A History of
## California Labor

## David F. Selvin

series editors:
Norris Hundley, jr.
John A. Schutz

430115
Boyd & Fraser Publishing Company
San Francisco

**A PLACE IN THE SUN:**
**A HISTORY OF CALIFORNIA LABOR**

*David F. Selvin*

© Copyright 1981 by Boyd & Fraser Publishing Company, 3627 Sacramento Street, San Francisco, CA 94118. All rights reserved.

Manufactured in the United States of America.

Library of Congress catalog card number: 81-66062

ISBN 0-87835-117-5

1 2 3 4 5 · 5 4 3 2 1

# EDITORS' INTRODUCTION

MENTION THE NAME CALIFORNIA and the popular mind conjures up images of romance and adventure of the sort that prompted the Spaniards in the 1540s to name the locale after a legendary Amazon queen. State of mind no less than geographic entity, California has become a popular image of a wonderful land of easy wealth, better health, pleasant living, and unlimited opportunities. While this has been true for some, for others it has been a land of disillusionment, and for too many it has become a place of crowded cities, congested roadways, smog, noise, racial unrest, and other problems. Still, the romantic image has persisted to make California the most populated state in the Union and the home of more newcomers each year than came during the first three hundred years following discovery by Europeans.

For most of its history Caifornia has been shrouded in mystery, better known for its terrain than for its settlers—first the Indians who arrived at least 11,000 years ago and then the Spaniards who followed in 1769. Spaniards, Mexicans, and blacks added only slightly to the non-Indian population until the American conquest of 1846 ushered in an era of unparalleled growth. With the discovery of gold, the building of the transcontinental railroad, and the development of crops and cities, people in massive numbers from all parts of the world began to inhabit the region. Thus California became a land of newcomers where a rich mixture of cultures pervades.

Fact and fiction are intertwined to well into the state's traditions and folklore that they are sometimes difficult to separate. But close scrutiny reveals that the people of California have made many solid contributions in land and water use, conservation of resources, politics, education, transportation, labor organization, literature, architectural styles, and learning to live with people of different cultural and ethnic heritages. These contributions, as well as those instances when Californians performed less admirably, are woven into the design of the Golden

State Series. The volumes in the Series are meant to be suggestive rather than exhaustive, interpretive rather than definitive. They invite the general public, the student, the scholar, and the teacher to read them not only for digested materials from a wide range of recent scholarship, but also for some new insights and ways of perceiving old problems. The Series, we trust, will be only the beginning of each reader's inquiry into the past of a state rich in historical excitement and significant in its impact on the nation.

Norris Hundley, jr.
John A. Schutz

# CONTENTS

*for Liz and Adam*
*with love and hope*

# FOREWORD

THE WAGE WORKER is a unique product of the industrial revolution. Without capital, seldom owning even the tools of his trade, his opportunity to earn a living depends almost totally on others. When he works, it is "for the good and at the command of another." His living is buffeted, interrupted, dictated by forces often beyond his reach. He is lashed by necessity to heavy, dirty, unsafe jobs, his margin of choice narrow and limited. He lives in or close to poverty.

The wage worker reacted to the harsh terms of his life in the industrial society in many ways—not least by joining in unions with those who shared his experience, his defeats, his hopes; and by using his political franchise, singly and collectively, though often erratically, inconsistently, spasmodically, in efforts to better their conditions.

From these wellsprings has emerged a center of power, one among many in our society. Many hate it and reject it; others support it and rely on it. Political powers court it. Industrial leaders deal with it or fight it. Some see it, according to where they sit, as short-sighted or visionary, conservative, liberal, or radical; as too powerful or too weak.

These pages sketch how it happened in California.

## CHAPTER ONE

# The Roots

## The Crushing Weight

INDIAN LABOR built the foundations of a society whose marks are to be seen even today; yet no workers in all the years of California history have been more tragically exploited. Whoever were their masters—Spanish, Mexican, or American—their lot was hunger, disease, violence, and death in crushing weight.

In the beginning, the Roman Catholic Church and the Spanish colonists intended conversion and mission labor as a prelude to self-reliance and eventual freedom. The earlier, gentler ways of recruiting soon gave way to sterner measures. Before the eighteenth century had ended, forced labor became the economic base of the mission system. When the Indians fled the mission, as countless thousands did, they were tracked down and forcibly returned.

Indian workers helped to clear land and erect buildings. They cultivated crops, tended herds, tanned hides, manufactured soap and candles, ground flour, and worked in leather and iron. They learned the skills of the shoemaker, bricklayer, carpenter, and blacksmith. Women spun, wove, and cooked, but they also worked at guarding stock and felling timber. Children, too, were put to work at an early age.

The Indians received no pay, only their daily food, a roof over them, and, once a year, a small allowance of clothing. Crop failures, along with the neglect of the missionaries, sometimes left them with less food than necessary to sustain themselves. Even harsher, however, must have been the unending conflict, as the University of California scholar S. F. Cook saw it, between the Indians' tendency to work in their native ways and the compulsions of the missions' economic life.[1] In their native environment, they had worked only as need or season dictated: bursts of work interspersed with periods of ease or play. Regular, daily work had little meaning for them; they had difficulty finding reason or purpose in their daily tasks. Author-artist Louis Choris, who visited them in 1816, noted their "fretful and thin" appearance. "They constantly gazed with sadness at the mountains which they can see in the distance."[2]

Their labor, forced or free, undergirded an economic empire of impressive dimensions. By the 1820s, twenty-one missions stretched from San Diego to Sonoma with an Indian population of some 64,500. They were surrounded by acres of gardens, vineyards, and orchards. They tended great herds of cattle, horses, sheep, swine, goats; raised seventy thousand bushels of wheat annually, along with maize, beans, fruit, vegetables; produced wine and brandy, soap, leather, hides, wool, oil, cotton, hemp, and linen. Their assets, said historian Zoeth S. Eldredge, ran into the millions and their annual returns were "enormous."[3]

In the Spanish scheme, the lands and livestock of the missions were ultimately to be distributed among the neophytes. Their service in the mission was to prepare them for the freedom to pursue their own lives. When the missions were secularized beginning in 1833, the Mexican Congress intended the assets to be turned over to the settlers and the Indians. But secularization invited only looting and plunder by those in official positions. Missions and presidios fell into ruins. The land, often extended by huge new grants, ended up in the hands of the *rancheros*. They took over the profitable hide-and-tallow trade they had shared with the missions. They took over hundreds of mission Indians as their own work force and came to rely on their unpaid labor. When labor was short, they sent armed posses into the Indian villages to recruit more. "The impression is gained," says Cook, "that capturing, or perhaps, better, kidnaping, had grown to the dimensions of a major industry by 1848."

Soon, the non-mission Indians—those who still wandered the interior hills and valleys—faced the coming of the gold-hunters. Under the impact of their invasion, the Indians' homes, clothing, and tools of the chase were destroyed; they were driven from the lands, streams, and forests they had so long used. "Never before in history," wrote Stephen Powers in a government report of 1877, "has a people been swept away with such terrible swiftness."[4]

Killing, disease, and starvation—"as a public or private enterprise," Cook observed—took a cruel toll. The Indian population of California when the padres first arrived, Cook estimates, was some 300,000. By the time of the Gold Rush (1850) it had fallen to 100,000; by 1860 to 35,000; and by 1880, to 23,000.[5]

# The New Work Force

THE DISCOVERY OF GOLD on the American River in 1848 stripped San Francisco of virtually its entire work force—the nearly five hundred who lived and worked in the somnolent, little village. Word of the discovery spread rapidly through California and, before many months had passed, leaped the continent and vaulted the seas: "All came rushing in a body," wrote Guillermo Prieto, "every man forcing a way for himself with weapons or naked fists to the fields of the Sacramento where through the water like flakes of a sunbeam sparkles the metal with which they sought to forge a key to happiness."[6] Miners spread across the Sierra foothills in waves of hundreds, then thousands, peopling the pastoral quiet of the northern interior with a giant, sprawling mining camp.

Some who landed at San Francisco never left. Many returned: the few who struck it rich, the others who found little more than hard work, privation, sickness, and disappointment. More thousands poured in. Some among them recognized in mining and miners vast new markets, even more valuable than gold; others simply welcomed the work. From them came the new economy of California and the labor force to work it.

Stores sprouted in the diggings. Freighters hauled supplies

from San Francisco, brought back gold. Wholesalers rounded up the supplies, tapping at first nearby areas, then, by ship and overland, the eastern seaboard and markets abroad. Herds of cattle were driven in from Texas, sheep from the southwest and Mexico. Lumber was shipped from Puget Sound, later from the north coast. Market gardens flourished and wheat ripened in the central valleys. "Soon," historian John W. Caughey noted, "the city by the Golden Gate was not just a point on the supply lines of the goldhunters, but the metropolis to which the entire interior, the mines included, became tributary."[7] Shipbuilding and ship repair yards, lumberyards, docks, flour mills, bakeries, and breweries sprang up. Stores, hotels, restaurants, houses of every kind were built (and rebuilt, as fire repeatedly mowed them down). Streets—made "impassable, not even jackassable" by winter rains—were graded and planked. Mining was the business of most Californians by far, but close to a third—more by the end of the decade—made their living as merchants, traders, laborers, craftsmen, farmers, and financiers.

Prices zoomed to unheard-of heights. A one-time U.S. Navy chaplain, returning to San Francisco in 1848, paid $6 for breakfast, he recalled, $50 for a new pair of boots, and $4 for a haircut and shave, with dull shears and a razor stropped on the barber's boots. An eating house offered low-grade hash for 75 cents, "18-carat" for $1; two potatoes, 75 cents; peeled, $1. Eggs sold at $1, $2, even $3 each, coffee at $4 a pound. A loaf of bread was 50 cents (a few pennies in the East), meat $3 a pound. "Good" board ran to $30 a week; "the most indifferent," $20. Rents were equally high; a little house of four rooms rented for $400 a month. Stores brought from one to six thousand dollars a month. Rooms at hotels ranged from $25 to $250 a week. The cost of living, commented historian Caughey, was "frightful."

Labor, too, was in short supply and wages were correspondingly high. "The daily laborer," the *Annals* reported, "who had worked for the good and at the command of another, for one or two dollars a day, could not be restrained from flying to the happy spot where he could earn six or ten times the amount. . . . The mechanic, who had been glad to receive two dollars, now rejected twenty for his day's services."[8]

Deflation of the unreal prices—and wages, too—left in the

wake of the Gold Rush was both inevitable and painful. Supply fluctuated wildly, prices often plummeting disastrously every time a ship docked. Merchants and traders reached out to new resources, nearby and afar, to meet the metropolis's consumer and capital needs. Competition sharpened. Gold production slowed, spreading unemployment and financial distress along the once optimistic streets.

Thousands of workers had responded to the goldfields and their promise of unbelievable riches. The tight, virtually closed labor market pushed wages for every kind of work to undreamed-of levels. Workers continued to flood in—jobhunters drawn by higher pay than they had ever known, unsuccessful prospectors, seekers of wealth, independence, adventure. Not only Chinese, but workers of many origins and skills were imported by frustrated employers intent on breaking the tight labor market. Newcomers happily took work at wages that were often below locally prevailing levels but which were also several cuts above any they had known in the East or abroad. Employers translated competitive pressures into lower wages and stretched-out hours. Workers came to know quickly that they faced rapidly narrowing choices, if any, beyond what was offered.

Across the country at mid-nineteenth century, the notion of union was stirring. A Massachusetts court had partially lifted the opprobrium imposed by earlier rulings that had labeled unions "unlawful conspiracies." The early ugly impact of the "wage system" sent some workers looking for utopian escapes. Some responded to cuts in pay or longer work-hours in spontaneous walkouts. Others turned to trade unions of weavers, printers, tailors, hatters, shoemakers, and cigarmakers. Before the 1850s had ended, a half-dozen national unions, evidencing some significant degree of local organization, had been formed.

Attitudes among San Francisco's gathering work force were clearly influenced, too, by the special character of work in the goldfields. Whatever their origins, goldhunters there found dignity and status. As an outgrowth of the crude democracy of the diggings, Bayard Taylor wrote, "the practical equality of all the members of a community, whatever might be the wealth, intelligence or profession of each, was never before thoroughly demonstrated as in San Francisco." Summing it up "in three words," Taylor declared, "LABOR IS RESPECTABLE."[9] The mining country's "practical equality," though, had limits. The goldhunters laid waste the Indians' way of life. Chinese were victimized by economic discrimination and violence. Mexicans and other Latins were tolerated, frequently exploited, while blacks were seldom accepted. Color often barred them from owning or working claims. They, along with the Chinese and Indians, were denied the right to vote or to testify, as witness or victim, in court.

This was the climate in which the new work force developed and grew: the crude and flawed democracy of the diggings, the ideas and expectations imported from a continent or even half a world away; the necessities imposed by a turbulent, volatile, expanding, and often oppressive economy. Workers asserted their interests with vigor and insistence to meet soaring living costs and to resist deflation's inexorable weight. They struck. They organized unions. They sought legislative redress. Union organization and labor legislation came to this newly minted town with surprising speed and intensity.

In November 1849 house carpenters in San Francisco struck for higher wages, followed a few days later by the carpenters in Sacramento. Early in 1850, printers formed the San Francisco Typographical Society in a successful effort to substitute piece rates for a weekly rate of pay—an effective increase in earnings. (The Society survives today in the Bay Area Typograpical Union, Local No. 21.) It was also the last time in several decades that the printers won a raise. By 1860, their rate of pay had been cut by seventy percent—from an effective rate of about $16 a day to less than $5. Nearly all trades in San Francisco organized during the 1850s: teamsters, draymen, lightermen, riggers, and stevedores in 1851; bricklayers and bakers in 1852; blacksmiths, plasterers, brickmasons, shipwrights, carpenters, and caulkers in 1853. Musicians, who had called a strike against the ceremonies in 1850 celebrating California's admission into the Union, reorganized in 1856 and struck again for union scale.[10]

Few of the organizations in these years lasted very long; none survived beyond the decade without reorganizing at least once. Repeatedly, workers saw their unions shattered in their first confrontation with their employers. But the impulse to organize survived, seemingly undiminished and at times enhanced, even in the face of unrelenting employer opposition.

Workers were introduced at the same time to the unemployment that would become a bitter fact in their work lives. In
1852, a relative newcomer wrote his wife, "There is more
people in this country that is out of money and destitute than
any country I was ever in."[11] That winter, historian Ira B. Cross
reported, found destitution and unemployment widespread, relieved the following spring when many left for the diggings. "It
is not always the case," the *Annals* noted later, "that the appli-
cant can find constant employment at his particular trade. However . . . he may always fairly calculate on finding employment as
a laborer in coarse work, or in doing odd jobs, at from $3.50 to
$5 a day." Gold production dropped sharply in the mid-1850s;
glutted markets, falling prices, and business failures rolled up
into what the *Annals* called a "commercial depression." The
*Alta California* estimated in 1856 that some three thousand
men were out of work in a city of about fifty thousand.

Such were the beginnings: high wages and high prices, deflation and unemployment, the almost instinctive reach for organization.

# A Bruised Reed

THE THRUST OF THE Gold Rush had in large part spent
itself by the end of the decade. The romantic flannel-
shirted figure of the 49er, bent over his pan, was fading from
the scene. Dynamite and heavy equipment, deep mines and
large-scale hydraulic operations—and wage-earners—were taking over the business of mining gold. The young state, especially
San Francisco, faced the uncomfortable realities of a lopsided
world, heavily weighted with mines and miners, lacking in capital, industry, and workers.

Shock waves from the development of the Comstock Lode in
1859 turned the economy in new directions, fueling a growth no
less expansive than in the early years of the Gold Rush. Silver
mining, unlike placer mining, required heavy equipment and
enormous infusions of capital. Individual claim operators soon
gave way to stock company operations and triggered a raging

speculation in mining stocks. The burgeoning industry yielded a soaring demand for equipment, materials, supplies of every kind, and men. Its demand built the foundations of the industrialized economy that dominated San Francisco's life for most of the coming century.

The rising flood of silver translated into business for San Francisco. The city's iron trades were soon swamped with orders for quartz mills and other mining machinery. Construction, both business and residential, boomed. Demand soared as well for wagons and carts, woolen goods and blankets, flour, lumber, sugar, beer—for all the necessities of life and industry. When demand from the Comstock slacked off, it was replaced, even enlarged as mining expanded into other parts of the West and into the Rockies. Agriculture, too, fed the stream of demand. California was on its way to becoming a major force in the world wheat trade. Construction of the Central Pacific was being pushed eastward over the Sierra in a race against the track gangs of the Union Pacific, working westward.

People continued to pour in. The state's population sailed past the half-million mark by 1870; San Francisco's population, 56,802 in 1860, climbed rapidly to 149,473 in 1870. The labor pool, though, remained shallow and workers found the labor market good. The Civil War, drawing heavily on the nation's available labor supply, added still greater protection from competition. Booming industry, a vigorous mining development, railroad construction, and expanding agriculture—all competed for the available labor supply.[12]

Workers responded to good times with a surging renewal of union organization. Unions quickly established themselves in San Francisco's metal trades, shipbuilding, and construction. Far more than other sectors of the city's economy, they were resistant to outside or national competition and found it easier to pass on higher costs to their customers. Their demand for higher skills also made replacement more difficult and recruiting strikebreakers a serious logistical problem. Workers in other industries—shoemaking, cigarmaking, woolen goods, clothing, for example—faced greater difficulties. Competition, from both local and imported goods, imposed ceilings on market prices and on labor costs. Skills in these industries were quickly developed and easily replaced. The combination made it possible, even encouraged, the introduction of easily exploited Chinese workers. Strongholds of white workers developed and survived in many of these industries but, by the end of the decade, Chinese workers made up major portions of their work forces. They became at the same time targets of an increasingly intense agitation and of legislation, both attempted and enacted, to exclude them from major areas of the economy—to defend white workers, their antagonists said, against competition of coolie labor.

Unions were organized and reorganized in a long list of trades and industries, stretching from bakers and boilermakers to shipwrights and waiters. Strikes flared. Many workers sought to recover wage cuts suffered in the late 1850s. Wages, the *San Francisco Bulletin* said in 1863, "were unreasonably low." Workmen were justified in seeking higher pay but, it added, "great care should be taken not to overdo the thing." Some, though, made other demands: painters wanted pay for Sunday work; bakers asked for a 12-hour workday and no work on Sunday; retail clerks campaigned for early (8 P.M.) store closings; bricklayers demanded an hour for lunch.

The flush of organization saw the formation in 1863 of the city's first central labor body, the San Francisco Trades' Union. By "uniting the Mechanics' Societies of this city," it provided broadened support for several striking unions. It voiced feelings about a number of political and legislative issues and took an active part in the developing campaign for the eight-hour day. Its brief life ended in 1866 in a petty dispute over conduct of the eight-hour campaign.

Employers organized, too, for combat more often than peace. Restaurant owners came together in 1861 for that purpose. Iron foundry employers formed an association in 1864 to resist a strike of molders. It lured strikebreakers from the East with advance passage and the promise of higher wages. Union representatives, however, intercepted the party at Panama and persuaded the newcomers to join the union. The employers conceded defeat.

Increasingly, though, working men focused their attention and energies on the eight-hour workday, a longstanding goal. In 1865, Alexander M. Kenaday, a veteran of army service in Mexico, a printer and a major figure in the city's typographical

union, and second president of the Trades' Council, spearheaded the campaign that presented the state legislature with an
11,000-signature petition calling for an eight-hour-day law. The
resulting bill lost, after a heated battle, by a single vote. The
defeat, though, spurred ongoing efforts to gain the shorter
workday by union action. Several of the shipyard trades had
initiated the eight-hour day earlier in the year; now, other crafts
set dates for installing it on their jobs. In January 1867, the
formation of the carpenters' Eight-Hour League brought fresh
troops to the movement. Under the leadership of A. M. Winn, a
one-time brigadier general in the state militia and a former
carpenter, the league stimulated activity in Oakland, Vallejo,
San Jose, and Sacramento, and as far away as Los Angeles.

Two thousand and sixty-six workers (according to the *Alta*'s
count) paraded June 3, 1867, to celebrate the achievement of
the eight-hour day. Marching in the order of their adoption of
the shorter workday were ship joiners, bricklayers, laborers,
lathers, riggers, gas fitters, house carpenters, and house painters.

Early in 1867 a workingmen's convention renewed the call
for an eight-hour law. The convention's short, but intense political life, alongside the spreading influence of the Mechanics'
State Council, won an eight-hour law from the 1868 legislature.[13] Employers strongly resisted the movement. They formed
a Ten-Hour Association and advertised in eastern papers for
men to work the longer shift. They resisted enforcement of the
newly enacted law. A State Supreme Court decision finally pin-
pointed its fatal flaw: nothing in the law prevented a worker
from "agreeing" with his employer to work longer hours.[14] Just
as the law proved a bruised reed, the workers' own developing
organizations, economic and political, were unable to withstand
the gathering storm.

## CHAPTER TWO

# The Conflict

## A Wrathful Response

**D**RIVING THE FINAL SPIKE in the transcontinental railroad in 1869 pushed San Francisco and the rest of California, for better or worse, into the larger world from which they had been so long separated. The torturous process sent shock waves through their society; cries of anguish and anger echoed ominously across the continent.

Californians had looked ahead expectantly to the day. As it approached, industry expanded, home tracts were readied, and farm land was subdivided. Employers, hopeful now of cracking the chronic labor shortage, advertised in the East a new bonanza of prosperity and plenty. Thousands responded—indeed began arriving a year ahead of time. The new day never dawned. Instead, San Francisco was engulfed by a tidal wave of economic disaster. A report by Samuel Bowles, in February 1870, in the Springfield, Massachusetts, *Republican,* described the first year of the railroad:

> All of the great interests of the State are depressed. Several thousand laborers are reported idle in San Francisco alone, and 50,000 to 100,000 in the State. Her great machine shops are nearly all still; building has ceased; real estate and rents are falling; the eight-hour leagues have crumbled to ash; and the manufacturers are either closing their shops altogether, or are successfully forcing their workmen to accept lower wages. . . . At first the people seemed stunned. . . . They cursed the railroad,

they cursed the Bank of California, and they cursed the Chinese, one and all, as parents of their disappointment.[1]

It got worse. The soaring Comstock silver boom crashed. The vaunted Bank of California collapsed. Drought struck the valleys and grain shipments slumped. Production in the city's machine shops and foundries dropped forty percent between 1875 and 1877, jobs by thirty percent. The papers estimated unemployment at 5,000 to 20,000, even at 30,000. The *Call* reported that "charities were feeding 1,400 persons a day." The *Chronicle* explained that "privation went far beyond hunger. Thousands were suffering from lack of food, but they could not withstand the cold either." Many, it said, had not "enough clothing to hide their nakedness."[2]

Frank Roney, an Irish rebel who emerged as a major figure in San Francisco's union movement, arrived in the city in 1875. In the diary he kept for a short time, he noted: "I began the year with very mild expectations, that of being out of debt by this time and of having my family, still increasing, better provided for. But, instead of clearing off my past indebtedness, I have added to it. And, while I still hope that another year will see me clearly out of debt, I confess I am somewhat doubtful." Roney diligently hunted for work, but jobs grew increasingly shorter and more intermittent. In January 1876 he wrote: "No money, rent due. Nothing coming from the room to help pay the rent. Coal nearly out. Little food in the house. And, worst of all, no prospects ahead. . . . God only knows what I will or can do under such circumstances." A week later, having earned just $2, he sold his tools. In February, he added, "the second month of this Centennial Year of Grace 1876 . . . I have earned $84.50 and produced 15 tons, averaging clear profit to the proprietors [of] $450."[3]

*Langley's San Francisco Business Directory* described it as an "extraordinary depression in almost all branches of labor; the city was thronged with a multitude of men out of employ such as had never before been known." Only relief and charity provided food and shelter for many of the city's people. Under the depression's dead weight, the union organization that had flourished in the 1860s collapsed. The eight-hour day, happily celebrated only a few years before by thousands of San Francisco workers, was wiped out, the ten-hour (and longer) day restored.

Widespread unemployment and continuing immigration finally ended the labor shortage that had characterized the city's first twenty years. Intensified competition from eastern manufacturers put new pressure on wages, pushing them inexorably lower. Historian Neil Shumsky summed it up: ". . . extreme poverty became common in San Francisco. Countless families lived at, or below, a bare subsistence level. Instead of a society in which everyone could better himself, industrialization created a class of men who struggled to survive."[4]

In this cauldron a sense of displacement joined the realities of deprivation. Immigrants, seeking places in American society, and older American stock, far from its eastern roots, suffered similar shocks of displacement. Even worse, they found themselves competing for livelihood with newcomers speaking in strange tongues. "Frustration," says Alexander Saxton, "replaced euphoria."[5]

Under the circumstances, social cohesion, as Carey McWilliams pointed out, could be quickly achieved by rallying opposition "to some 'menace,' real or imagined."[6] The Chinese had been victims of discrimination in the goldfields; San Franciscans tried repeatedly to legislate Chinese competition out of existence. They shared the outcast status of the Indian and the black: they were denied the vote and barred from testifying in court. They were blocked from many economic areas, pushed into the dirty, unwanted, and unskilled jobs, into low pay, sweatshop conditions, and tenement living. Shumsky estimated they made up 13.2 percent of the city's work force in 1870 and 15.5 percent in 1880. But he also counted more than 59 percent in the boot and shoe factories, 89 percent in cigarmaking, and between a quarter and a third in textile mills, clothing, and other light manufacturing. Culture and language remained barriers between them and their non-Chinese cohabitants. The conviction was virtually ineradicable among whites that Chinese by nature were satisfied with long hours and low pay, a bowl of rice, and a dank hovel. Blatant discrimination was sanctioned by widespread and deep-seated attitudes that equated racial differences with inferiority and unfair economic competition. The Chinese were a well-fitted "menace," close at hand.

Still another "menace" loomed: the millionaires who made fortunes in gold or silver or railroad profits and spent them in gaudy living. James C. Flood and William S. O'Brien, former owners of the Auction Lunch Room, used their Comstock millions to build richly furnished castles on Nob Hill. Mark Hopkins, one of the Central Pacific's Big Four, was building a "glorified, gingerbread, three-million-dollar castle" when he died in 1878. It looked, commented Gertrude Atherton, "as if several architects had been employed and they fought one another to the finish." Wealth led to greater wealth, greater power. The Big Four extended its railroad empire into the valleys and the length of the state. Leland Stanford served as governor and later as United States senator. Banker William Ralston made fortunes loaning money to Comstock mine and mill owners. Before his strange death in 1875, his wealth extended to a railroad equipment factory, woolen mills, a sugar refinery, and more. The new millionaires combined bad manners and ostentatious living, but neither manners nor wealth alone made them targets. It was their rapid and massive accumulation of economic power and political influence. They stood out in sharp relief against a landscape of unemployment and poverty, of displacement and disappointment.

The cauldron came to a sharp boil in July 1877, fueled by a series of railroad strikes in the East. The Workingmen's Party of the United States summoned the public to a protest meeting on the night of July 23 on the sandlots in front of the City Hall, then under "leisurely" construction. The meeting devoted itself to a peaceful denunciation of monopoly, capitalists, and railroads, but it broke up with a cry of "On to Chinatown." A cheering, jeering crowd raided a score of Chinese laundries, wrecked a plumbing shop mistaken for another laundry, and stoned the Chinese Methodist Mission; police finally dispersed the mob. Apprehensive "law and order" businessmen the next day formed a second Committee of Safety, headed by William T. Coleman, a merchant who had led the first vigilantes in 1856. Thousands responded to his call for volunteers. Within forty-eight hours, the new vigilantes were backed by offers of arms, U.S. gunboats were standing by, and some 1,200 militiamen were under arms. The raids resumed the next night with an attempted attack on the Mission Woolen Mills where Chinese made up a large part of the work force. A speaker on the third evening called for exterminating the employers of the Chinese and for blowing up the ships of the Pacific Mail, a major carrier of Chinese immigrants. In the rioting that followed, a "pick-handle brigade," backed by police, deflected an attack on the Pacific Mail docks. The mob instead set fire to a nearby lumber yard, then attempted to prevent fire fighters from trying to control the flames. The extraordinary show of strength by civil authorities effectively suppressed further outbreaks. The "pick-handle brigade" was disbanded soon after. Governor William Irwin blamed the disorders on hoodlums and thieves, "mere wantonness," and on "a small sprinkling of Communists or Internationalists who hope to usher in the millennium by a judicious use of the torch." But, he asked, if grievances went unrectified, how long would laborers forbear?[7]

From the riots emerged an unlikely leader. A onetime seaman turned drayman, Dennis Kearney, had been a member of the "pick-handle brigade." An ambitious man, Kearney had sought to improve himself in the Sunday night meetings of the Lyceum for Self-Culture. He was a frequent speaker, too, at the Sunday afternoon sandlot meetings. Frank Roney, no admirer, labeled him a "persistent buffoon," a failure. The Workingmen's Party of the U.S. rejected him; his current defense of workingmen clashed sharply with his earlier tirades against them. He helped put together the Workingmen's Trade and Labor Union which self-destructed in a dispute over campaign contributions. In October, though, he emerged as president of the newly formed Workingmen's Party of California (WPC). His speeches became increasingly vituperative, echoing the cry, "The Chinese must go" and attacking with mounting anger the "capitalists" and "money power." "I will give Central Pacific just three months to discharge their Chinamen," he said in one of his milder outbursts, "and if that is not done, Stanford and his crowd will have to take the consequences." In another outburst: "The dignity of labor must be sustained, even if we have to kill every wretch that opposes it."[8]

However crude, Kearney's appeal captured the anger and frustration of the victims of depression and industrialization. Thousands joined the WPC ward clubs that sprang up in virtu-ally every section of the city and spread rapidly to many parts of the state. Ethnic groups, trades, neighborhoods formed political organizations that gave the WPC almost overnight political power. Sandlot meetings, frequent club meetings, and political activities became an important focus in the lives of working people. Kearney was arrested, released, and rearrested, as one charge put it, for language "having a tendency to cause a breach of the peace." Both the San Francisco Board of Supervisors and the state legislature attempted to gag him, but they failed to discourage the WPC's steadily mounting following or its increasingly vigorous political action.

Despite a police effort to prevent it, the WPC met in convention in January 1878. The delegates announced one location, then met secretly in another. On the second day of the convention, Kearney won acquittal on one of his several arrests. By happy coincidence, too, the voters in Alameda County that day elected a WPC candidate to the state senate. The convention denounced Chinese cheap labor as "a curse to our land." Capitalists and their "willing tools" had taken over government and trampled the people's rights. The convention also called for a system of finance outside the reach of "rings, brokers, and bankers," urged an eight-hour law, prevailing wages on public works, and a tax system that would make monopolies impossible.

The WPC's growing support produced an impressive series of local election victories. Most notably, it elected a full third of the delegates to the 1878 state constitutional convention and, that fall in San Francisco, elected the mayor and a long list of city, school, and judicial officials. The party reached the peak of its influence that year. Kearney, his leadership increasingly challenged, soon after turned futilely to the national Greenback Labor Party. He continued his political activity for a time but without reclaiming the glory of old. In 1884 he quit politics to become a real estate broker.

Traces of the WPC's brief power linger in the state constitution, though much of its—and the constitution's—effort was rewritten later by the courts. It was anything but a workingman's constitution, Henry George declared, but it was radical enough to frighten, temporarily at least, the more conservative sections of the people. It authorized broad actions to curtail, if not end, the competition of Chinese workers, though virtually all of the restrictions ran afoul of treaty or constitutional barriers. It took measures to increase the accountability of corporations and banks, their directors and stockholders. It sanctioned

a state income tax. It brought the railroads and public utilities
under the regulation of the Railroad Commission, predecessor
of the present Public Utilities Commission. Of little use at the
outset, it became increasingly effective as a regulatory force in
the state's economy. It provided a constitutional basis for legislation dealing with mechanics' liens, the eight-hour day, and
convict labor. George described the document as a mixture of
"constitutional code, stump-speech, and mandamus," a barrier
to "future radicalism." Its opponents denounced it as "radical"
and "socialistic." Even so, the people approved it in 1879 by a
vote of 77,957 to 67,234.

In its short, turbulent life, the WPC echoed and amplified the
anger and frustration of the unemployed, the poor, the dis-
tressed, and the displaced. It lifted the long-agitated question of
the status of the Chinese to a national level. It was responsible
for updating the state constitution. It offered no long-term
measures or goals that might have coped with the workingmen's
problems of unemployment or impoverishment or eased the
abrasive impact of industrialization. It flared in a bright blaze of
demagoguery, anger, and hopelessness, demonstrated dramatically the possibility of political action, then died. It was, most
of all, a wrathful, bitter response to a glowering, increasingly
oppressive industrial society.

# "How Not to Combat Unionism"

T HE STRUGGLE TO ORGANIZE unions in the final quarter
of the nineteenth century, paralleled by the rise of com-
bative employer organizations, made conflict inevitable and
paved the way for the stormy climax that engulfed the city in
1901.

The battle was fought against a backdrop of soaring, if uneven, economic growth. Farm production, worth $60 million in
1880, climbed to $132 million in 1900. San Francisco's industry
expanded vigorously, but its gains were overshadowed in growth
by the rest of the state. Los Angeles, a town of 11,183 in 1880,
reached 85,407 in 1900, with some eight thousand wage earners

in its 1,500 manufacturing establishments. Oakland's factories employed about 4,000 workers, Sacramento's 4,200. Eighty-five percent of the nearly seven thousand new manufacturing establishments and three-quarters of the 47,000 additional workers were outside San Francisco.[9] Growth, though, stumbled from seasonal ups-and-downs into hard times, unemployment, crashing prices, and business failures, emerging again into prosperous times.

San Francisco workers fought to hold on to a part of their gold-rush wage advantage, though plainly the gap was closing. The average San Francisco factory worker earned $525 in 1880, about the same in 1900. His counterpart in the rest of the country earned $353 in 1880, $432 in 1900. Workers organized unions in twenty-four trades in 1882 or joined the twenty-five already in existence. They were reinforced by the Representative Assembly of Trades and Labor Unions (later the Federated Trades Council, and in turn the San Francisco Labor Council). Much of their energy was given to vigorous anti-Chinese (later broadened to "Asiatic Exclusion") activities, promoting boycotts of Chinese-made goods and often the merchants who handled them. But they also refined their techniques of utilizing boycotts in labor disputes, opening new sources of support for striking unions, and encouraging union organization.

Organized workers increasingly found themselves facing a rising tide of employer antagonism. An attempt in 1885 to impose a fifteen percent pay cut in the city's iron works provoked a month-long strike of some 1,400 workers and led to the formation of the Federated Iron Trades Council. Another attempted pay cut—this time on coastwise ships—led sailors to organize the Coast Seamen's Union. The new union was midwifed by a group of landlubber radicals who formed a shoreside "advisory committee" to run the union while its members were at sea. It quickly enrolled 2,200 members and successfully fought off the pay cut.

Employers, too, organized. Cooks and waiters struck to avert work rules drafted by the Eating House Keepers' Association. The iron trades employers, organized in the Engineers' and Iron Founders' Association, soon forced a long and bitter strike on the molders. The twenty-month dispute shattered the union. An association of boot and shoe manufacturers locked out its

union employees. The Millmen's Protective Association successfully opposed the eight-hour day. Other employer organizations developed among master bakers, cigar manufacturers,
brewers, retail shoe dealers, dry goods merchants, builders, and
master carpenters. The Ship Owners Association's demand for a
reduction in pay precipitated a prolonged strike, marked by
"violence and rioting." With the help of the hated "grade book"
and their own shipping offices, the shipowners effectively
screened out union supporters and "troublemakers." The grade
book provided prospective employers with the jobseeker's past
employment record, along with employers' "grades" on conduct, ability, and so forth. Unsatisfactory marks for whatever
reason (or no reason) virtually blocked future employment. An
explosion in front of a seamen's boarding house in December
1893 killed six outright, two others dying later. The crime was
charged to the striking seamen, effectively ending the dispute in
their defeat.

Employers with a work force of forty thousand in August
1891 organized the Board of Manufacturers and Employers of
California, seeking, it asserted, peaceful settlements of disputes.
But it launched what Ira Cross labeled a "campaign of extirpa-
tion." A treasurer of the association told a state investigation in
1892 that it had no objection to trade organizations, but it objected to "unreasonable, aggressive demands, boycotting among
others, and interfering with people's business, walking people's
factories without authority, talking to the men, . . . and interfering with a man's business in general." In 1893, the association
reported, "One after another the unions have been taught a
salutary lesson until out of the horde of unions only one or two
are left of any strength." A year later, it boasted that "among the
industries of San Francisco there remains but a single union
which imposes its rules upon its trade. The reason why this
union still continues to dictate terms is because the employing
printers have never combined to resist its demands."[10]

A booming prosperity greeted the new century, built on the
occupation of the Philippines, new and expanding industry, and
new commercial connections with Alaska and the Orient. It set
the stage for the showdown. The Labor Council, with fewer
than a score of affiliates in 1898, counted 90 in 1901. Labor
Commissioner F. V. Meyers in 1900 reported 20,000 union

members in San Francisco, 26 local unions with 2,100 members in Los Angeles, 23 local unions and 3,000 members in Oakland, 20 unions and a thousand members in Sacramento. The skilled construction trades had formed their own Building Trades Council in 1896 and, under the leadership of P. H. McCarthy, organized a dozen unions and were building a close-knit, cohesive organization. Unions were also extending their reach to many lesser-skilled workers as well as to the skilled craftsmen.

Early in 1901, a group of influential employers put together a new, this time secret, association—the Employers Association of San Francisco. They provided a war chest estimated at upwards of $250,000 and bonded themselves to stick together until the job was done. They gave a five-member executive committee a veto over individual employer and trade settlements and reinforced it with effective control over sources of supplies for the city's thousands of employers.

The new association showed its hand almost at once when the metal polishers left their jobs to gain an eight-hour day. Willing employers found themselves threatened with a loss of supplies if they gave in. The strike ended unsuccessfully some three months later. A thousand cooks and waiters struck on May 1, seeking a ten-hour day, a six-day week, and union houses in which only union members would be employed. They quickly signed up some three hundred smaller houses, but the larger ones resisted through a newly formed Restaurant Keepers' Association. Union houses quickly found themselves unable to obtain bread or meat from their customary suppliers. Bakers walked out in protest at many bakeries. A strike threat by meat-cutters persuaded retail meat dealers to continue supplying the union restaurants. Early in July, though, wholesale meat packers announced they would no longer supply retail shops that were furnishing meat to the fair restaurants. Some 1,500 butchers struck in retaliation but were unable to make their strike stick. Union house cards began coming down all around town. Carriage and wagon makers struck on May 8 to enforce an agreement on shorter hours and higher wages. If they put the agreement into effect, the employers were threatened with the loss of their supplies. Teamsters announced they would no longer haul goods for firms refusing to supply union shops. Two weeks later, the employers agreed to make the earlier agreement effective, but without a written contract. On May 20, the iron trades, involving some four thousand workers, struck for a nine-hour day. The smaller shops, which were willing to concede the shorter workday, faced the now-familiar threat. The strike continued for ten months.

In mid-July, the Epworth League convention came to town. The contract for handling its luggage had been given to a firm that was neither union nor a member of the Draymen's Association. When it appealed to a union firm for help in handling the job, Michael Casey, the teamsters' business agent, warned it would be a violation of their contract; the union would instruct its members to refuse to do the work.

The teamsters had organized just a year earlier. One employer who attempted to oust the union was hit with a short, effective strike. Other draymen, though, saw an opportunity to stabilize labor costs in a fiercely competitive business and signed a two-way closed-shop agreement. They agreed to hire only members of the union and to refuse to help any nonunion firm. In return, the union agreed its members would not work for any operator not a member of the association. Faced with the Epworth League situation, the draymen were not only encouraged but pushed into challenging the union by the Employers' Association which had established a new merchants' drayage company, apparently as a warning to draymen to stand firm.

Under orders from the association's executive committee, one drayman after another fired teamsters who refused to haul the luggage of the Epworth League. Within a week, some 1,300 teamsters had been locked out. The union met the challenge by calling out the rest of its 2,500 members. Draymen replaced them with farmhands fresh from the country, recruited college students and discharged soldiers returning from the Philippines, and imported black workers to drive the drays. Hoots and jeers gave way to stones and fists. Mayor James Phelan hired 200 extra police and put them on the wagons to protect the strikebreakers and, the union said, to guide them around town and help handle the freight. The dispute spread: to hay teamsters, to bottlers, to porters, packers, and warehousemen—to workers anywhere who refused to load or unload wagons driven by strikebreakers.

An employer spokesman said, "No conference with the unions

has been proposed and none is expected." The Labor Council turned for reinforcements to the City Front Federation. The Federation claimed 13,000 members in 14 local unions and a treasury of over $250,000. On July 29, it voted to call out its full membership in support of the teamsters. Waterfront workers in San Francisco were joined by workers in Oakland, Redwood City, Benicia, Crockett, and Port Costa, as well as workers in building materials and coalyard teamsters, and more—some 15,000 in all. Ships were idled in the harbor as fast as they arrived. Wheat shipments, mounting toward their seasonal peak, were halted. To the farmers' complaint that their wheat would rot, the employers replied, "Let it rot." Repeated attempts at negotiations and appeals from Mayor Phelan, the board of supervisors, and leaders of civic and small business groups were turned aside. The employers said they were waging a battle for their right to run their businesses without interference from organized labor. Governor Henry T. Gage turned down a request from the chamber of commerce for state militia. Violence mounted. Before the dispute ended, five deaths, 336 assaults, and hundreds of arrests were recorded. To union protests against police violence, Mayor Phelan reportedly replied, "If they don't want to be clubbed, let them go back to work."

Governor Gage came to San Francisco on October 2, 1901, and met with the leaders of the draymen, the teamsters, and the City Front Federation. Within hours, he announced that an agreement had been reached—its terms were never made public—and all strikers would return to work the next day.[11]

It was no victory for the unions but their sheer survival was a clearcut defeat for the employers. Their campaign to demolish or weaken fatally the city's unions, commented historian Robert E. L. Knight, ended in a debacle.[13] The teamsters regained their contract in 1902. The Sailors Union won its first formal agreement with the shipowners. The cooks and waiters won union conditions. By the spring, the Labor Council reported 130 affiliated unions. The strike cleared the way for a renewed upsurge of unionism. It ended for a time effective employer opposition and gave way to two decades in which San Francisco became known as the nation's strongest union town.

"It was an example," reporter Ray Stannard Baker summed up later, "of how not to combat unionism.'[13]

# The Potential of Political Action

I N AN ANGRY AFTERMATH to the great strike, a solid plurality of San Francisco voters in November 1901 took control of the city government in the name of labor.[14] Their political triumph owed much to widespread resentment against Mayor James Phelan's near total surrender of the police to the employers' cause. In office, some unions contended, labor could prevent the police from being used to protect strikebreakers and do the strikers' work. The building trades, particularly their iron-fisted leader, P. H. McCarthy, opposed the idea of a political movement based on "class." "I found that we had a class government already," replied Andrew Furuseth, the sailors' leader and a major figure in the City Federation. Principal leaders in the Labor Council were reluctant but the teamsters and waterfront unions supported the new Union Labor Party.

Eugene Schmitz, a union musician and the Union Labor Party candidate, was the new mayor. Three of the party's candidates were elected to the board of supervisors. Schmitz was reelected in 1903, and in 1905 he and his entire Union Labor Party slate were swept into office. With its overwhelming success, the party, under the manipulations of a wily Republican lawyer, Abraham Ruef, put up the city and its privileges for sale, reaping a golden harvest of dishonest dollars. The corruption, suspected before the 1906 earthquake and fire interrupted it, was dragged into the open by the graft prosecution that followed the disaster. The revelations destroyed the party and it was turned out of office.

But not for long. In 1909, ironically, the name and remnants of the party came under the control of McCarthy, who had opposed it so strongly in 1903 and 1905. He used it to win the mayor's office in 1909, but he was defeated in 1911 and again in 1915, ending the party's existence. (The name survives today in an endorsing organization representing a small number of local unions.)

These were not, by any means, labor's first ventures into political waters. Repeatedly, from the Gold Rush days on, workers had turned to political action to voice their resentments and to seek remedies for the ills that troubled them. Both as independent voters or organized in political union, they often looked to government action to provide safeguards and benefits in a rough-handed industrial society.

In July 1850, San Francisco teamsters asked the board of supervisors to protect them against what they considered the unfair competition of Australian teamsters. An attempt to reinforce their political goal by putting up a candidate for the board split the new organization. The board, nevertheless, enacted an ordinance prohibiting aliens from engaging in draying, driving hackney coaches, or rowing boats carrying passengers. In another political flyer, a notice in the *Alta California* in 1851 warned workingmen that a judge seeking reelection was an unsuitable candidate in view of his decision rejecting a wage claim lodged by some laborers, but he won reelection nevertheless. And in 1852 the pleas of bakers were apparently responsible for an ordinance forbidding sale of bakery goods on Sunday—an indirect effort to abolish Saturday night and Sunday work.

On becoming president of the San Francisco Trades Union, the city's first central labor body, in 1865, Alexander M. Kenaday spearheaded what became a vigorous campaign, in the legislature and on the job, for the eight-hour day. By mid-1867, the *Morning Call* reported, "the fact exists that the eight-hour system is more in vogue in this city than in any part of the world, although there are no laws to enforce it."

The 1868 legislature passed the first eight-hour law. It also enacted a comprehensive mechanic's lien law—the first, Lucile Eaves wrote, "entirely satisfactory to the working people." It offered workers a priority claim for their pay against the assets of bankrupt, defaulting, runaway, or simply crooked employers. The original law had been enacted in 1850 and amended, almost session by session, until the action of the 1868 legislature. The eight-hour law proved to be, in Alexander Saxton's phrase, "a lawyer's trick" as hard times in the 1870s blotted out the eight-hour day on the job.

Behind these tentative legislative successes was an alliance linking unionists, a citywide organization of anticoolie clubs, and the Democratic Party. The ward organization and detailed political apparatus developed by the anticoolie organization provided a pattern which was repeated frequently in the years

ahead. Notably it was repeated in the organization and skyrocketing rise of the Workingmen's Party of California. Anti-
Chinese agitation, alongside workers' demands for protection
against economic exploitation and unemployment, provided
basic elements of political effectiveness. It won a wide range of
political victories, not the least its success in electing a major
bloc of delegates to the constitutional convention of 1878–
1879. Its triumphs were tentative at best; the new constitution,
as noted earlier, was less than an overwhelming success.

The potential of political action was glimpsed briefly in the
electoral victories that put the Union Labor Party in San Francisco's City Hall. Workers' concerns echoed prominently a few
years later in the rise to power of the Progressive party under
Hiram Johnson in 1910. They were given concrete expression
in an unprecedented flood of protective labor legislation, measures extending the people's political reach, and in the appoint-
ment of labor representatives to prominent and unaccustomed
places in state government.

The initiative and referendum gave California voters a new
independence and a new authority in influencing legislation. The
recall provided a check on elected officials, including judges.
Women gained the right to vote. The poll tax was ended. The
Railroad Commission was given new powers to deal with the
vast economic power of the Southern Pacific, a principal butt of
Progressive anger, and with the rapidly growing influence of
public utilities.

The Progressive years saw the enactment of a comprehensive
scheme of workers' compensation for industrial injury or death.
It overthrew generations of legal doctrine that had protected
employers against claims for compensation of maimed workers
or of the dependents of workers killed on the job. The new law
made compensation insurance mandatory and assured the
worker compensation without regard to the risk he may have
assumed by taking the job, his own contributory negligence, or
that of a fellow worker.

A labor demand for an effective eight-hour law, backed by a
petition with 90,000 signers, passed the assembly but died in
the senate. The California State Federation of Labor subsequently adopted the Samuel Gompers doctrine that the shorter

workday was best obtained by union organization and economic action. That stand, however, did not interfere with the passage in 1911 of a law limiting women workers to eight hours' work in a day, forty-eight in a week. In 1913, California became the eighth state in the nation to adopt a minimum wage law covering women and minors. Labor leaders, some of whom joined business in opposing the measure, argued the minimum would inevitably become the maximum. ("An erroneous prediction," later observed Paul Scharrenberg, who at the time was secretary of the State Federation of Labor.) It would, they contended further, undermine wage standards and remove any incentive to seek better conditions by joining a union. Supporters pointed to subsistence-level wages as low as ten cents an hour and to their disastrous effect on women workers' health and morale. The new law created the Industrial Welfare Commission— Walter Mathewson, a union sheet-metal worker from San Jose, was made a member—to establish a minimum wage on the basis of the comfort, health, safety, and welfare of working women and minors. Studies in 1914 showed that over half of the women working in major industries received less than $9.63 a week, found to be the minimum cost of living for a self-dependent woman worker. The IWC's first wage order in 1916 set a minimum rate of 16 cents an hour.

The uncertain legal status of unions themselves at the time provided additional incentive for political concern. In general, workers were lawfully entitled to strike. They were equally entitled to use "peaceful persuasion" to support their walkout. As Eaves pointed out, "this concession is not great, since the means and opportunities are held subject to injunctions." Union labels to advertise goods made under "fair" conditions had not been restricted, though the use of "unfair" labels, as in a boycott, had been held unlawful. California unions (like American unions generally) and their activities were lawful according to the means employed and the purposes pursued. Judges decided which means and which purposes were "lawful," using injunctions to enforce their views. Labor was unable to outlaw the "yellow dog contract," requiring a worker to agree, as a condition of being hired, that he would not join a union. The boycott, again subject to the courts' views of the means and purposes, was usually lawful. Picketing, often viewed as "inherently illegal," was later subjected to even greater restraint. No sanction was provided in statutory law for unions as such or for their necessary activities.

# The Forty-Five-Year War

I RONICALLY, Harrison Gray Otis had been for a part of his working life a member in good standing of the printers' union. As a fifteen-year-old "devil," he is said to have quit his job at the *Rock Island Courier* when the proprietor refused to allow the union in his shop. He had been a member, too, of the Columbia Typographical Union in Washington, D.C. After acquiring the *Los Angeles Times* in 1881, he maintained for a time friendly, even helpful, relations with the Los Angeles Typographical Union. But he became not merely a union-hater but the dominant spirit, a vigorous advocate, an aggressive leader in a forty-five-year battle to establish and maintain the antiunion open shop.[15] He used without stint the thundering voice of the *Times* and his rapidly swelling wealth and influence to advance the cause of what he called "industrial freedom."

The turning point came in 1890 when he locked out the union printers on the *Times* to enforce his demand for a twenty-percent wage cut. Joined at first, then abandoned, by publishers of the other three Los Angeles newspapers, Otis fought on alone. He succeeded in establishing the open shop on the *Times* and, despite a long, stubborn, often bitter boycott, in maintaining it. He devoted his energies, too, to organizing what at the outset was a defense of the open shop but soon became a virulent offensive against unionism.

Otis's angry vendetta fitted hand in glove with the developing vision of Los Angeles as the focal point of a great southern California agricultural-industrial empire. The vision had thrived briefly in a high-flying real-estate boom in the late 1880s. Excursion trains had brought thousands of tourists to see for themselves the land, the cheap homes, and the opportunities that had been promised. Many came in search of the health-giving benevolence of the climate. Businessmen, practicing and prospective, were lured by the smell of prosperity, and workers by the prospect of jobs. Some came simply to escape the harshness of eastern winters.

The boom—one of the wildest in the history of the United States, the *Times* said—collapsed after little more than two years. From its shambles, business leaders with Otis in the van organized the Los Angeles Chamber of Commerce. Otis called it the "new beginning." It soon undertook an increasingly aggressive and systematic campaign to recruit workers, homebuyers, and businesses. In these schemes, the promise of the open shop—a large pool of labor, available at low wages, uncluttered by union organization—was an indispensable prerequisite. That promise was especially vital if Los Angeles were to compete effectively against the giant to the north—San Francisco—where unions and high wages were increasingly prominent in the cityscape.

The victory of the open shop did not come easy. Workers in the city's growing industry had tried repeatedly to organize from the time in 1875 when a handful of printers formed Local 174 of the International Typographical Union. Other workers tried to follow the printers' example. Their efforts were speeded by the boom, frustrated and repelled by its collapse. Local 174 itself was caught in the whiplash when its members were driven from the *Times*'s shop by an angry, purple-faced Otis. The new century found labor weak, disorganized, with neither stability nor achievement to show.

Los Angeles was no longer the village it had been twenty years before. Pressed by the boom and by the "new beginnings," its population had multiplied seven times to 85,407. The census counted 1,415 manufacturing plants in 1900; it had not bothered to count them in 1880. Its manufacturing work force had doubled in just ten years to 8,044. The value of its output had climbed to $21.1 million, more than twice what it had been ten years before. Los Angeles still lived in the shadow of San Francisco, but its growth was explosive. In 1896, two major organizations of employers had combined to form the Merchants' and Manufacturers' Association. By 1900 the M&M was wheeled into the front ranks of Otis's battalions in the war against unions.

In 1900, and again in 1907 and 1910, the American Federation of Labor sent in representatives to help workers organize unions. Their efforts drew the full blast of the open-shop armament: blacklists, ads recruiting "independent" workers, imported strikebreakers, firings and lockouts, and cancellations of union contracts. The M&M and Otis provided beleaguered employers with financial and moral support and put heavy pressure on employers dealing with unions. The unions managed, just barely, to hold on in the face of the heavy employer attack.

The decisive battle opened in 1910. A theatre boycott gave unionists fresh hope. A new AFL organizer spurred recruiting efforts, especially in the building trades. Other national unions sent organizers to help in the fight. Brewery workers walked out in May. Metal trades workers called a strike on June 1. The M&M recruited strikebreakers and provided vigorous support for the struck employers. By now, San Francisco unions had become deeply involved. With wages in Los Angeles twenty and thirty and even forty percent below those in the north, San Francisco unions began to bump hard against their competition. In the spring, San Francisco metal trades employers demanded equalization of wages and hours up and down the coast, threatening to withdraw their contracts, including the eight-hour day. The labor councils of San Francisco and Alameda counties, the local and state building trades councils, and the State Federation of Labor organized the General Strike Committee, called for contributions of twenty-five cents per member, and sent ten organizers of their own into the fight. Los Angeles employers fought back with a sweeping antipicketing ordinance that became a model for employers up and down the state. Strikes and strikers were hit with widespread injunctions and arrests. The employer offensive pushed the unions into an increasingly closer alliance with the Socialist Party that produced the Union Labor Political Club. It named Job Harriman, a lawyer and Socialist leader, as its candidate for mayor, along with a number of unionists as candidates for the city council. In the primary a year later, Harriman showed surprising strength in leading the way to a runoff. By September 1910 the Central Labor Council's membership was up by half from the start of the year.

Early in the morning of October 1, an explosion and fire

devastated the *Times* plant, killing twenty employees.[16] Unexploded dynamite, with faulty alarm clocks attached, was discovered later that day at the home of Otis and of Felix J. Zeehandelaar, secretary of the M & M. *Times* officials, almost within the hour, accused labor of the crime. Union leaders indignantly denied any implication. Union printers offered their help in returning the *Times* to publication.

The unexploded dynamite eventually put William J. Burns, head of a detective agency prominent in labor disputes, on a trail leading to James B. McNamara, a union printer; his brother, John J., secretary of the Bridge and Structural Iron Workers; and Ortie McManigal. McManigal provided Burns with a detailed account of the *Times* bombing. He also implicated scores of unionists across the country in the Iron Workers' bitter and often violent fight against the antiunion campaign of their employers, the National Erectors' Association. With AFL president Samuel Gompers leading the way, labor denounced the arrests as a "frame-up"; thousands of union members in every part of the country contributed to the fund to defend the brothers. Clarence Darrow, a famous fighter in labor cases, headed the defense when the trial opened on October 11, 1911. On December 1, the brothers appeared together in court for the first time. Observers were stunned to hear them reverse their reiterated pleas of innocence. John accepted responsibility for the *Times* bombing and James for the dynamiting of the Llewellyn Iron Works in Los Angeles on Christmas Day 1910. James was sentenced to fifteen years and John to life in prison.

The brothers' shocking turnabout shattered the labor front that had grown up in their defense. Undoubted belief in their innocence gave way to humiliation and defeat. It gave fresh credence to the sweeping charges of force and violence that were stock weapons in the open-shop arsenal. "Industrial freedom," exulted the *Times* a few weeks later, "reigns supreme."

The McNamaras' confessions ended the twenty-one-month campaign against the open shop in Los Angeles. It had, until then, produced twenty-two new local unions and enrolled over ten thousand new members. The promising, new political alliance that only a few weeks before had led the way to a surprising primary election victory was "swept into oblivion." The committee went out of business soon after, noting that it had spent $334,000 in its efforts. The metal trades strike ended after twenty-one months with small gains but without the eight-hour day. Organizing came to a halt, membership declined, and militancy waned. Employers held on to their low-wage advantage: machinists told the U.S. Commission on Industrial Relations in 1914 that their wages were 15 to 25 cents an hour below those in union towns. Building trades were paid $1 to $2.50 a day less than in San Francisco and worked nine and ten hours a day instead of eight. In a report on the commission's hearings in Los Angeles, John A. Fitch summed up: "The term 'open shop' [in Los Angeles] is wholly a misnomer. It is as tight a closed-shop town as San Francisco—with the lock on the opposite side of the door. Employers on the stand frankly stated they would not employ union men."[17]

The open shop almost totally dominated Los Angeles industry for the next twenty-five years. Unions clung to a scant toehold; organization flared from time to time, especially during the years of World War I. But the area's enormous industrial growth over those years—until halted by the Great Depression—took place almost entirely under open-shop conditions. Unions flourished in the newborn oil industry during World War I only to sink into inactivity until roused in the 1930s. Organization came to movie backlots in 1926 and screen talent searched for effective representation, one of the few areas where unions actually gained recognition during the open-shop reign.

In 1929, the *Times* chose October 1, anniversary of the 1910 bombing, to inaugurate a month-long series of articles recounting what it headlined "Story of Forty-Year War for a Free City." "For the war is neither over nor won," it said. "The forces, which for four decades, have sought by strategy and violence to enchain the industries of Los Angeles are far from being beaten or discouraged by their long series of reverses." It argued that the open shop has been "of chief importance in bringing about the phenomenal industrial growth of Los Angeles." Of fifteen labor disputes it considered "major," it claimed none had been successful. Only one vocation, it said, could be described as wholly unionized—that of the musicians—and it was "not properly an industry and, at that, not one indigenous to Los

Angeles." As the series neared its end, it shared front-page space with other ironic headlines: "Stock Market Madhouse in Terrific Price Crash," "Stocks Dive amid Frenzy in 16,410,000-Share Day."[18]

# A New Army of Workers

WHEAT, LIKE GOLD, opened the way to an empire of unimagined affluence. It also brought into being a new army of workers, the forebears of today's farm work force. Like its industrial counterpart, it had neither tools nor capital nor property, and it was dependent for its living on wages, paid by and according to the convenience of another. Henry George described the early recruits in 1871: "and over our ill-kept, shadeless, dusty roads, where a house is an unwonted landmark, and which runs frequently through the same man's land, plod the tramps, with blankets on back, the labourers of the California farmer, looking for work, in its seasons, or toiling back to the city when ploughing is ended or the wheat crop is gathered."[19] From them in an unbroken line have descended the invisible thousands—the "blanket" or "bindle" stiffs, the Wobblies and the hoboes, the Chinese and Japanese and Filipinos and Mexicans, the "Okies" and "Arkies"—who planted, cultivated, and reaped the harvests whose yearly value today climbs beyond $6 billion.

California agriculture grew up outside the American tradition of family farms, multiple crops, and independent farmers. It was initially shaped by the land-grant pattern of Spanish and Mexican landholding. The huge grants found their way, by force, guile, and law, into the hands of American owners. The bonanza wheat ranches gave way to orchards and vineyards and in turn to expanding acreages of highly specialized, diversified crops. To work them, they needed large quantities of relatively unskilled labor in short, seasonal bursts and always at the lowest possible cost. For the workers that meant intermittent, short-run jobs and low wages. Even the most mobile were fortunate if they could find work in much more than half the months of the year. Large holdings, specialized crops, increasing quantities of capital investment, worked by a highly transient, economically dependent force of laborers created, in Carey McWilliams's apt label, "factories in the fields." The inexorable result for the farm workers was built-in, chronic poverty.

Minimal investments of capital and a quick return produced a new "bonanza" in wheat. Large tracts of land and gold-rush-inflated wages encouraged mechanization. The initial work force of Indians and Chinese was replaced by multishared plows, horse-drawn, then power-operated harvesters and farm machines. They were operated by a transient army of disappointed miners, evicted squatters, and unemployed city workers. Their situation was reflected, McWilliams noted, in the 1886 proceedings of the State Agricultural Society: "Our nomadic herds of farm hands must have all the year employment and an abiding place with their work; they must be fed and housed as civilized men should be fed and housed; the wide gap between employed and unemployed must be closed."

Exhausted lands, falling returns, and increased competition turned the wheat ranches to more profitable, better-suited uses of the land. Fruit orchards, vineyards, dairy farms, and citrus groves led the way to the increasingly specialized crops that soon became the hallmark of California agriculture. Extended railroad construction and the development of ice plants and refrigerated freight cars opened distant markets. Irrigation, pressures of growing population, and rising land prices encouraged intensive cultivation. By the turn of the century California's farms were producing a quarter of the nation's canned fruits and vegetables, ninety-five percent of its apricots, two-thirds of its prunes and plums. The new specialized crops, no less than the wheat ranches before them, required a similarly cheap, mobile, temporary, and abundant labor supply.

Chinese made up a large part of the farm work force in the latter years of the old century. Intimidated by the white community, the Chinese workers found a measure of protection in their associations or "tongs." Rarely heard of, says a California Bureau of Labor Statistics report in 1888, but "in case of a strike or boycott they are fierce and determined in their action, making a bitter and prolonged fight." On the farms, the tong served more as an employment agency, a forerunner of the labor contractor system, than as a collective bargaining agency. They were driven from the farms in the 1890s and replaced in turn by Japanese immigrants, Hindustani, and Filipinos. The pattern remained fixed: it was often only a case of which group was in the poorest, least defensible position. "No one in the state," wrote John W. Caughey, "gave serious thought to the problem of the itinerant."

Until, according to Carleton H. Parker, an impressive event took place in August 1913: "an unusual strike, as strange as any in the annals of western labor. Men were killed, the country side cast into hysteria, the militia called out. . . . With the dramatic entry of the hop pickers on the stage there began such a widespread and agitated discussion of the condition of the state's casual workers, that the two years of 1913 and 1914 will be known in western labor history as the 'period of the migratory worker.' "[19]

Nearly 2,800 hop pickers, including many women and children, had responded to ads for workers at the Durst ranch at Wheatland. They were camped on a treeless hill, some in tents or in topless squares of sacking; many made their beds on piles of straw under the open sky. No provision had been made for sanitation or garbage disposal; dirty waste water collected in stagnant pools around the grounds. Eight "revoltingly filthy" toilets served the entire community. Drinking and cooking water was scarce. Only a limited number were allowed to pick each day. They discovered that water was unavailable in the fields, though they could buy lemonade peddled by a cousin of the ranch owner. The owner was also cut in for half of the profits of the grocery concession in the camp. The advertised "bonus" proved to be a "hold-back" from the picker's earnings; it was paid only if the picker worked the full season.

Among the pickers were perhaps a hundred members of the Industrial Workers of the World, the Wobblies. Two of them, Blackie Ford and Herman Suhr, were prominent among those who undertook to organize a protest. The ranch owner rejected the committee's request for improvements, provoking "a more or less involuntary strike" which climaxed in a protest meeting that drew close to a thousand pickers. As Blackie Ford spoke to the crowd, a sheriff's posse drove up. With guns and revolvers, it tried to disperse the crowd and arrest Ford. A shot rang out, then a tattoo of firing. Two pickers, a deputy sheriff, and

the district attorney of the county were killed. The National
Guard was brought in, a manhunt unleashed for the fleeing
Wobblies. Many of them were tracked down and arrested, with
little regard for due process, and tried for the Wheatland murders. Ford and Suhr were sent to prison.[20]

The headlines, perhaps for the first time, told Californians of
the plight of the state's migratory workers. The "agitated discussion" that followed resulted in creation of the state Commission
on Immigration and Housing, whose mission was to improve
living conditions in migratory labor camps. Under its aegis,
Carleton Parker's investigations provided a close-up view of
existing conditions. But the attention dwindled and other generations were condemned to live through these conditions in
their own times.

Parker estimated in 1913 that the pickers had come to Wheatland from three sources: a third were "town casuals," men and
boys from nearby cities and towns; another group were "quasi-
gypsies" with carts or ramshackle wagons; a final third were the
"migratories—pure hobo, or his California exemplar, the 'fruit
tramp'; Hindus; and a large body of Japanese." Mexican workers had begun to join the farm work force before World War I,
and in 1920, McWilliams, says, more than half of the harvest
was gathered by Mexican workers. Their numbers steadily increased, the *Pacific Rural Press* estimated, to an average of
58,000 each year between 1924 and 1930. Growers sought
federal help in importing workers, but one added, "Keep them
out of our schools and out of our social problems." When limits
on Mexican immigration were proposed, growers imported Filipino laborers, young, single, womenless men, whose numbers
reached 30,000 by 1930.

Farm workers made several efforts to organize in the pre-
Depression years but none of the organizations survived. At the
same time, growers were fashioning even more effective con-
trols over their labor supply. They formed labor exchanges to
act for them in estimating labor requirements, fixing wages, and
recruiting help. McWilliams estimated that growers' labor costs
fell ten to thirty percent with the inception of the exchanges.
They shared the expenses of recruiting, relieved individual
growers of any responsibility for the workers, made it easier to
create a controlled labor surplus, and to meet current labor

needs. Wages, too, were dropping in the last half of the 1920s. The La Follette Committee of the U.S. Senate, looking back on the decade noted "an almost complete cessation of effort by the general public through the state government to ameliorate working and living conditions through protective legislation. It was, in fact, a ten-year lull before a storm."

# "The Lowest and Darkest Depths"

FOR NEARLY TWO DECADES after the 1901 teamsters' strike, San Francisco was a union town—Ira Cross called it "the only closed-shop city in the United States." In 1916, the employers returned to the attack. In the next half-dozen years, reinforcing their undoubted economic power with political strength, the employers shattered the closed shop, weakened or destroyed countless local unions, and imposed an iron-fisted open shop on the city's workers. For a long, bitter decade, the open shop under the imposing label of the "American Plan" held sway.

A newly formed Merchants' and Manufacturers' Association, backed by employer organizations in neighboring cities, launched the attack. The combined forces waged a six-month— and ultimately victorious—battle against culinary workers, retail clerks, and construction workers in Stockton. A longshoremen's strike on the San Francisco waterfront in mid-1916 opened a new and, as it turned out, critical conflict.

The longshoremen claimed they needed a wage increase to meet rising living costs. The employers accused them of violating an agreement they had signed the year before. When the teamsters refused to support them and the employers started bringing in strikebreakers, the longshoremen suddenly ended their walkout. Violence erupted, however, between the union men and the strikebreakers who had been retained on the job. When the employers refused to fire the strikebreakers, the longshoremen walked out a second time.

The second strike drew cries of outrage from the San Francisco Chamber of Commerce. Its president, Frederick J. Koster, told a meeting of nearly two thousand businessmen that it was time to stamp out "that disease permeating this community." The new Law and Order Committee pledged to maintain the "right to employ union men or non-union in whole or in part" and collected a war chest of $200,000 within minutes, a million dollars ("in round figures") soon after. The city's major businesses, such as shipping, lumber, rails, oil, and banking, backed the committee. The waterfront employers put the longshoremen's strike in its hands. By July 17, four days later, the longshoremen once again returned to work.

Five days later, as a noisy Preparedness Day parade made its way up Market Street, a bomb exploded at Market and Steuart streets. It killed ten and wounded forty persons. On July 26, invoking "shades" of the vigilantes, the Law and Order Committee convened a mass meeting in the Civic Auditorium presumably as a protest against the bombing. But to Koster, it was "another expression of the disease" the committee had been formed to combat. In short order, the police arrested Tom Mooney, his wife, Rena, Warren Billings, and two others, charging them with the Preparedness Day murders. Mooney was a radical organizer who had been involved in several labor disputes and had been arrested (though acquitted) on charges of possessing illegal explosives. Billings, a union activist, too, had been sent to prison after being found with a suitcase of dynamite during a Pacific Gas and Electric strike in 1913. Billings was imprisoned for life and Mooney sentenced to death. His sentence was later commuted to life imprisonment after protests that were heard across the continent and overseas. The convictions of the two men proved, in time, to be the product of "hysteria" of the moment, outright perjury, manipulated evidence, and incompetent witnesses.[21]

A strike and lockout of culinary workers served the Law and Order Committee as launching pad for an antipicketing ordinance, modeled after the Los Angeles measure and banning virtually every kind of picketing. "There is no such thing as peaceful picketing," Koster declared. The committee packed its message into an intensive advertising campaign, capped by a four-hundred-women telephone drive. The ordinance passed. Under its ban, a flurry of injunctions quickly broke the restaurant strike.

With the coming of World War I, the labor-management

battle was briefly set aside. War industries, a measure of government support, and a sharp rise in consumer prices combined to produce gains in union membership and wages. Once the overseas hostilities ended, the domestic battle resumed with renewed ferocity.

Longshoremen served demands on the employers not only for higher pay but for participation in "the ownership, profits, and directorates" of the companies. Employers wheeled in battalions of strikebreakers and launched an intensive campaign aimed at the "radical" leadership of the strike. From the often-violent dispute emerged the "Longshoremen's Association of San Francisco and the Bay District" (known in time as the "Blue Book" union, in contrast to the red dues book of the old). It was formed by a group of walking bosses (working foremen), longshoremen believed, under the employers' directions; no man could work, it was understood, without approval of one of them. It dominated the waterfront for the next fourteen years. The decimation of the independent longshoremen's union was followed in 1921 by the destruction of the seafaring unions; unionism on the sea survived only in a handful of coastal "steam-schooners." The decisive battle in the employers' open-shop drive, though, was fought in San Francisco's up till then tightly organized building trades.

Under P. H. McCarthy's formidable leadership, the Building Trades Council had become the dominant force in the city's construction industry. It enforced its rules on employers, individual local unions, and union members alike. It banned non-union workers and nonunion materials from the jobs. It outlawed jurisdictional strikes and restriction of output. It took over, almost totally, the bargaining functions of the local unions but refused to deal with any organized group of employers. The arrangement protected the workers' job opportunities against lower-paid, nonunion competition; provided employers a skilled work force; and assured them guaranteed and uniform labor costs. Under its sway, wages stayed relatively stable from 1907 to 1917, but rising living costs soon generated strong pressures for wage increases. In 1920, with four unions on strike and a general walkout looming, an agreement was reached to submit the unions' demands for pay increases to arbitration. While the arbitration board had the case under consideration, the country endured a short, sharp depression and prices plummeted. On March 31, 1921, the board ordered a 7½ percent pay cut. The unions angrily argued that the board had no power to cut wages; the only question before it had been the increases. Their refusal to accept the award was met with an industry-wide lockout. The employers, now organized in the Builders' Exchange (overriding McCarthy's refusal to deal with a multiemployer organization), were backed by the old Law and Order Committee in new dress and by the mobilized support of building materials suppliers, bankers, and other employers. When the council finally voted on June 10 to accept the award, it was told that the union members could return only under open-shop conditions.

The Industrial Association, successor to the Law and Order Committee, implemented the open shop. With a sizable war chest and widespread support among the city's businessmen, it opened hiring halls, recruited nonunion workers, and provided training schools. It utilized a permit system to bar union contractors' access to building materials; it had at least a tacit agreement of the banks to refuse them credit. A number of crafts, from time to time, challenged the almost total domination of the open-shop employers, but without substantial success. Unions survived but they lost influence in setting wages or working conditions. Their banners hung unused in virtually empty halls.[22]

David Warren Ryder, no admirer of San Francisco's union environment, wrote the obituary in 1926: "The open shop obtains in virtually all the principal industries of the community. . . . From eighty to ninety percent of the manual labor of San Francisco is now done under open shop conditions." From "the prize union labor city of America," he wrote, San Francisco had fallen to "the lowest and darkest depths."[23]

## CHAPTER THREE

# Turning Point

## Overthrowing the Open Shop

**A**MONG ALL THE depressions the United States has suffered," historian Irving Bernstein observed, that of the 1930s "is the only one we elect to call 'great.'" It was "unique," he thought, for sheer size and for its complete unexpectedness, but most of all for its overwhelming "experience in joblessness."[1] At its depth—on that snowy day in March 1933 when Franklin Delano Roosevelt took his oath as the nation's president—some 15 million Americans, possibly more, were out of work—almost one of every three in the nation's work force. Most had been jobless for months, many for years. Those who clung to their jobs suffered, two, three, and more wage cuts. Falling prices helped to ease the pinch, but job opportunities and work hours also fell and wages in some cases dropped below subsistence levels.

A San Francisco grocery clerk remembered that wages were cut from $40 a week to $15, or $16 if married. E. E. Ellison, formerly in the office of the Sailors' Union, wrote to Ira Cross in 1932: "Our warehouse at 6th and Berry streets has two open sheds with concrete floors. Nightly about twenty men sleep on the concrete." When he asked why they did not apply to a Salvation Army shelter, he was told that, to get a bed for the night, one had to line up in early afternoon. And a man was not welcomed for a second night. A longshoreman wrote to the underground *Waterfront Worker:* "...how do we live? Well, some of us who are married work for the Charities and get in return, food that in most cases could not be sold on public markets, and for this rotten chuck we must work every third week." Germain Bulcke, a retired longshoreman, told a *San Francisco Chronicle* reporter fifty years later that he scavenged ruined vegetables from the produce market or gathered spillage from broken cases on the docks. "Of course," he added, "sometimes we'd make sure a case or sack broke."

The right to organize and bargain collectively, committed to law for the first time in Section 7a of the National Industrial Recovery Act of 1933, gave workers hope. A San Francisco union official remembered groups of workers walking the halls of the old Labor Temple looking for a union to join. But the open-shop, antiunion stand of the employers across the country was still strong. More than three times as many workers walked out in strikes in 1933 than in the year before and even more walked out in 1934. By far the most important issue was the right to join a union and bargain collectively.

All of the angers and fears and abuses of the depression years, the unyielding domination of the open shop and the "American Plan," the hopes aroused by the Roosevelt beginnings seemed to come into focus on the waterfront—not of San Francisco alone, though it became the principal arena, but in San Pedro, in Portland and Seattle, in dozens of smaller ports up and down the Pacific Coast. Oppressed for years by the employer-dominated "Blue Book" union, longshoremen in San Francisco broke away and joined the International Longshoremen's Association; dockers along the entire coast followed suit. The newly revived union won a test battle on Matson's San Francisco docks, effectively burying the remnants of the "Blue Book" and opening the way to the crucial conflict that rocked the coast and the nation in the summer of 1934.

The longshoremen's demand mirrored the evils that had accumulated under fourteen years of employer domination. The union's proposed hiring hall would replace the morning dock-side shape-up and end the no-holds-barred job competition; defeat bribe-seeking bosses and the usurious loan rackets; and eliminate the feast-or-famine job distribution that allowed a few crews nearly unlimited hours and limited the work of a far greater number to a few days or hours. They called for a pay increase and shorter basic hours. The employers evaded the issue: they could not bargain in San Francisco for the entire coast, they said; the closed shop was un-American; the union leadership was "Communist."

On May 9, from Seattle to San Diego, some 12,000 longshoremen walkd out. They were joined in the days that followed by thousands of sailors and firemen and stewards, masters and mates and marine engineers. Backed by the still powerful Industrial Association, the employers attempted to negotiate an agreement over the heads of the longshoremen and their local leaders. It was ingloriously overridden by the ranks of the strikers. The attempted agreement also ignored the other striking maritime unions, an omission that was emphatically underscored when negotiations passed to a newly formed Joint Marine Strike Committee, headed by the longshoremen's rising leader, Harry Bridges. The strike was reinforced, too, when teamsters extended their boycott of the docks to all cargo handled by strikebreakers.

Negotiations in the first two months of the strike had been carried out to a counterpoint of employer-stimulated demands for opening the port, whatever the cost. The employers, working with the Industrial Association and the police, speeded their preparations. On July 3, a parade of trucks, convoyed by police and guards, rolled out from Pier 38. Pickets greeted it with jeers and bricks; police retaliated with clubs and tear gas. The conflict raged up and down the waterfront the day long while trucks continued to roll. Next morning—the Fourth of July—the employers proclaimed the port open. But hostilities resumed early the following day—a day that went into waterfront legend as "Bloody Thursday." Again the battle swarmed over the Embarcadero, up and down Rincon Hill, rocks and brickbats against tear gas and, finally, firearms. When the day ended, two men were dead. That afternoon, Governor Frank Merriam ordered the National Guard to patrol the San Francisco waterfront.

A funeral march of ten thousand strikers and sympathizers, eloquent in its silence, buried the two men. First the teamsters, then one union after another voted for a general strike. On the morning of July 16 tens of thousands of workers left their jobs. Trucks and cabs disappeared from the streets; Market Street's four ranks of streetcar rails stood shiny and empty. Grocery stores were quickly emptied of their stocks. Filling stations closed. Day by day, the pressure of the strike gradually eased, until it ended on the fourth day. From it emerged an agreement to arbitrate the key issues in the longshoremen's dispute and a commitment by the shipowners to recognize and bargain with the unions chosen by the various units of maritime workers. On August 31, the waterfront and maritime strikes ended. The National Longshoremen's Board mandated a jointly operated hiring hall for longshoremen, but with a union-selected dispatcher as a safeguard against discrimination or favoritism; a basic, six-hour workday; and a wage increase. In time, other waterfront and seafaring workers completed contracts covering their jobs.[2]

The waterfront and general strikes dramatically symbolized the rush to organize unions across the country. Workers flooded into existing unions or, where there was none, created their own. In San Francisco longshoremen, seeking to defend their flanks, launched an organizing campaign among warehouse workers—a drive that came to be known as the "inland march." Where no warehousemen had carried a union card in 1933, nearly nine thousand were covered by union contracts by 1938. Workers organized unions in supermarkets and department stores, hotels and restaurants, machine shops and construction jobs.

The open shop, however, was not yet dead. The Industrial Association struggled on for a time, using labor spies, operating its nonunion employment bureau, recruiting strikebreakers when needed, issuing antiunion propaganda. Some of the familiar open-shop figures were seen in the Committee of 43, successor to the Industrial Association. It sought through public hearings to bend public opinion toward the employers and through private study to recommend correction of "any unsatisfactory conditions" that might attract union organization. It yielded in turn to the San Francisco Employers Council, formed in 1938 to assert the employers' "right" to bargain collectively. "Master" agreements, often industry-wide and covering expanded geographical areas, came into use to protect employers from being whipsawed in company-by-company negotiations.

The multiemployer, expanded-area contracts soon covered a large majority of Bay Area union workers.

The depression had treated Los Angeles no more gently than it did San Francisco or any other American cities and towns. In 1931, county officials registered more than 200,000 unemployed workers, offering them, skilled and unskilled alike, to public works at the common laborer wage rate of $3.20 a day. Between the depression and the open shop, the city's union movement was little more than a skeleton. Yet, moved by the soaring spirit of the Roosevelt times and despite a quarter-century of domination by a thoroughly organized, well financed, and highly sophisticated open shop, workers flooded into unions. But the fight for recognition and for stature was long and hard.

The Merchants' and Manufacturers' Association, vigorous and well-heeled, met the recovery program and its promise of union rights with its customary open-shop response. It advised employers to refuse to bargain or even to meet with union representatives. Nothing in the National Recovery Act, it contended, required employees to join, or employers to deal with, labor organizations. NRA compliance agencies were helpless in dealing with the spreading employer resistance.

M&M continued to pour hundreds of thousands of dollars, collected from auto and tire companies, public utilities and banks—the very cream of Los Angeles business—into its anti-union activities. It recruited strikebreakers. It provided the police with generous funds to strengthen its already close ties, paying huge sums for guard duty in private disputes and supplying quantities of tear gas. When the U.S. Supreme Court upheld the Wagner Act, guaranteeing union rights, the M&M not only resisted but encouraged defiance of the law. In a renewed offensive, Southern Californians, Inc. was organized as a "general staff" to take over the M&M propaganda campaign. It set up an "Employees Advisory Committee" to form employer-dominated company unions. It organized The Neutral Thousands (TNT) to combat what it called "the wave of industrial disaster." Women of the Pacific, purportedly an organization of housewives opposed to monopolies and rackets, encouraged violation of picket lines and shopping at struck businesses. Though these organizations claimed to be independent, the La Follette Committee (a subcommittee of the U.S. Senate Committee on Education and Labor under the chairmanship of Senator Robert M. La Follette, Jr.) found that Southern Californians, Inc. and the chamber of commerce financed their activities. The committee concluded: "The most influential business and financial interests in Los Angeles have attempted to sabotage the national labor policy of collective bargaining." The committee cited the use of labor spies, professional strikebreakers, arms and tear gas, and blacklists as well as a variety of "third-party" pressures as devices for bending law enforcement against unions and persuading employers to maintain open-shop policies.

Nevertheless, workers continued to organize. "The year 1940," said labor historians Louis and Richard Perry, "was the first one to see Los Angeles labor in a position to exert a significant influence, by reason of its own strength, on the community's economic and political affairs."[3] The unions claimed half of the city's work force was union; the employers discounted it to forty percent. In either case, Los Angeles's image as the "white spot" of the open shop had been heavily, if not fatally, damaged.

# A Closer Look

THE DRAMATIC UPSURGE of union organization in the 1930s was reflected in rising wage rates, reduced hours of work, and a greater voice in governing the workplace. The union movement won broader recognition, too, as government during World War II acknowledged its key role in war production. A sharp outburst of industrial conflict in the early postwar years, coupled with enactment in 1947 of the Taft-Hartley amendments to the Wagner Act, restricted labor's economic weapons and redirected its political orientation. By 1950, the unions directly represented a near peak proportion of the labor force and probably spoke for an even larger part. Midcentury provides a useful vantage point for a closer look.

California's work force in 1850 had been dominated by mining and miners. Explosive economic growth and steadily mounting in-migration had molded it by the turn of the century into something more closely resembling the national labor force. Changes over the next fifty years roughly paralleled national development but, by 1950, it had developed its own peculiarities.

It had, for one thing, a significantly higher proportion of white-collar workers than the national labor force, 45 percent against 37 percent. The proportions in San Francisco and Los Angeles were even higher, hovering around the fifty percent mark. California's blue-collar work force was smaller than the national proportion—a larger percentage of skilled craftsmen, but smaller proportions of operatives and laborers. Service workers made up a larger part of the state's work force than of the national. Agricultural occupations represented one-sixteenth of the state's labor force, while they were one-eighth of the national.

Of California's 3,209,000 wage and salary workers (excluding farm workers) in 1950, 42 percent belonged to unions.[4] Over the preceding fifty years, union membership had multiplied by some twenty times, which was three times as fast as the state's skyrocketing population. Compared with the national union movement (in 1956), California unions had larger proportions of construction crafts, service workers, and employees in retail and wholesale trade. Half of the nation's union members worked in manufacturing but only a third in California. In general, workers in manual occupations—skilled crafts, factory workers, transportation—were widely and heavily organized. On the other hand, white-collar workers in finance, insurance, real estate, and many service industries were only lightly organized or not at all.

Geographically, Los Angeles in 1954 held the largest concentration of union members; its 688,300 members made up 44 percent of the state's 1,566,000. Thirty-three percent (517,300) worked in the San Francisco Bay area. Penetration, however, was substantially deeper in the San Francisco area where unions represented two-thirds of the wage and salary workers compared with 40 percent in Los Angeles. Other clusters of union members were located in the San Joaquin Valley, San Diego, and the Sacramento Valley.

Neither growth nor the pattern of labor relations over the

years was the product of straight-line development. Initially, the individual employer faced a union of his own employees. The union was usually reinforced in time by employees in competitive firms in the same or similar crafts or trades. In the San Francisco area, particularly, but in other areas, too, employers organized to meet the broader organization of their employees— at first, to combat organization, later to bargain on more equal terms. The launching of the San Francisco Employers Council in 1938 signaled a trend from the single-employer contract to broader-area, multiemployer agreements. Union contracts in the Bay Area, noted economist Clark Kerr, more completely covered eligible workers than in the nation as a whole. Notably, too, three-fourths of Bay Area union members were covered by multiemployer contracts, 55 percent of those in Los Angeles, 32 percent nationally.[5]

The development was accentuated in the building trades. Individual contracts when unionism returned to the construction industry soon gave way to far broader systems of collective bargaining. Agreements in some cases were stretched over statewide, multistate, and even national jurisdictions. Regional contracts were negotiated within the state for five basic crafts covering, for example, forty-six northern countries or a dozen southern counties. Other contracts covered several counties. The extended reach of the bargaining undoubtedly contributed to virtually one hundred percent organization in the state's construction industry.[6]

Teamster organization in San Francisco and Oakland (and, most helpfully, in Seattle as well) revived briskly under the impetus of Section 7a of the National Industrial Recovery Act. The 1934 waterfront strikes and the rapid rise of unions in related industries spurred organization. The Los Angeles open shop withstood the pressures for several years until it was breached in the latter half of the decade by a combination of renewed organizational strength, particularly in the Bay Area, and the unionization of over-the-highway trucking. "Hot cargo"—that is, freight handled by nonunion workers or strike-breakers—from the open-shop, nonunion trucking operators found access to unionized areas and union lines increasingly difficult. Southern California open-shop forces moved in solidly behind Pacific Freight Lines when it faced a showdown with the teamsters. In the end, though, the pressures from union areas and by union members helped to win a key contract from PFL, tearing a great gap in the open-shop defense of Los Angeles trucking.

On the waterfronts, the end of the 1934 strike launched a new battle in detail over job conditions. Short, sudden walkouts—"quickie" strikes—renewed the battle, dock by dock, at times port by port. They struck to exert some control over the conditions under which they worked. They resisted efforts of the bosses to "speed-up" the movement of cargo between ship and shore. They walked out if they felt the number of men was inadequate to the job or cargo. They quit work when overly heavy slingloads forced the pace of work beyond what they considered fair. Safety on the job was frequently an issue. In all, according to one study, approximately 1,300 such local stoppages took place between 1934 and 1948, as well as twenty major port strikes and four coastwide strikes. Over 200 arbitration awards defined the rules and interpreted the contract. Waterfront employers responded in large part with an attack on union leadership; the union accused them of seeking a return to the old patterns of exploitation. After a ninety-five-day strike in 1948, a "new look" settlement wrote into the contract many of the work rules and procedures carved out in the fourteen-year battle.[7] But now, new issues came to the fore.

Employers were especially frustrated by the longshoremen's resistance to new machinery and labor-saving methods. Workers feared new methods would wipe out their jobs or, at least, limit their ability to improve their living standards. A mechanization and modernization agreement in 1960, painstakingly negotiated over several years, was intended to clear the way for automation of cargo-handling in return for a share in the anticipated savings. Old work rules painfully pieced together over the preceding quarter-century were now discarded. Two basic conditions governed the work: it must be safe and it could demand only a reasonable workload and workpace. In return, longshoremen were to receive a share of the savings in the form of guarantees against lay-offs and against any reduction in earnings. Money incentives were offered to encourage early retirement.

"Things worked out very differently," Lincoln Fairley, a long-time research director for the longshoremen's union, says. Gains in productivity were "enormous," he found; labor cost per ton dropped sharply, even after substantial rises in pay and benefits. The Vietnam war, moreover, produced unanticipated increases in tonnage and, despite enormously increased productivity, in manhours. As a result, the guarantees against layoffs or loss of earnings went unused. The longshoremen's direct participation in the savings consisted of a "vesting" benefit payable on retirement at age sixty-five and the payout in 1966 of the unused wage guarantee fund. A second five-year agreement replaced the wage guarantee with an extra pay raise and additional vesting benefits. Ironically, a sharp upsurge in containerization cut available manhours and reduced earnings, creating the very situation the now-discarded wage guarantee had been designed to meet. The guarantee was restored in 1972 and pensions were improved. Mechanization made work easier, Fairley concluded, and "West Coast longshoremen continue to enjoy a unique degree of lifetime security."[8]

By midcentury, Los Angeles's manufacturing had far outdistanced that of the San Francisco Bay area. Its work force was now double that of San Francisco. Los Angeles assembly plants produced 154,000 cars in 1941, more than 600,000 by 1949. Unionization came relatively early, too, as part of the auto workers' drive toward national contracts. The aircraft industry had climbed from a thousand employees in 1933 to a wartime force of 280,000. Custom-made airplanes gave way under wartime demand to mass production, a situation ready-made for industrial unions. Efforts to organize the new work force, however, ran into difficulties when the CIO and the AFL assigned the task to rival unions—the CIO to the auto workers, the AFL to the International Association of Machinists. They clashed sharply and frequently in the competition to win the support of the aircraft workers. Nor were unions welcomed in an industry so recently graduated from individualistic engineer-operators and hand-crafted production. Its attitudes were bolstered by the prevailing open-shop policies of southern California industry. Union organizers ran a seemingly endless gauntlet of company-wide associations, independent unions, intensive antiunion campaigns, and "hard line" bargaining. Nor was the newly recruited work force, unaccustomed to union ways, an easy audience. Company by company and plant by plant, major producers were brought under union contract. Government pressures during World War II and the national labor laws helped to create a more comfortable clime for collective bargaining. Mutual assistance pacts later eased the interunion rivalry.[9]

Unionism came relatively early to the movies, not southern California's largest industry, by any means, but among its best known. The producers signed a basic studio agreement in 1926 with unions representing the back-lot technicians, craftsmen, and other production personnel. Hollywood talent, however, was left in the care of the Academy of Motion Picture Arts and Sciences, later far better known for its annual "Oscar" awards than for its representation of the actors, writers, directors, and others. At the first opportunity they deserted the academy for their own guilds. Affiliation of the movie producers with expanding national chains of theaters and of back-lot technicians with projectionists and other theater personnel counterbalanced southern California's open-shop pressures. Producers, too, enjoyed a measure of freedom from local sources of supplies and credit.

The largely casual employment of back-lot workers made the unions major sources of skilled workers and, in turn, gave great importance to jurisdiction over the jobs. It produced continuing interunion warfare, complicated by corruption, political ideology, and union strategy. Producers, no idle spectators, intervened with favor and pressure to resolve the conflict in their own best interests. A National Labor Relations Board ruling in 1949 assigned the International Alliance of Theatre and Stage Employees extensive jurisdiction over many of the contending crafts. Concentration in one international union offered a means of resolving job conflicts without the studio wars that had formerly resulted.[10]

Other unions developed their own patterns of labor relations. From a strong, largely New Deal–inspired base in San Francisco, the Service Employees (then the Building Service Employees) set out after World War II to organize workers in Los Angeles. In an often bitter, employer-by-employer campaign, opposed frequently by the women's and shopper organizations spawned by Southern Californians, Inc., it gradually widened its toehold. It gained strength when it successfully organized hospital workers and, later, when it became the state's largest union of public workers. Retail clerks, with local unions scattered around the state, gained impetus from its prewar and immediate postwar contracts with Safeway Stores. Tandem bargaining during and after World War II helped to bring the smaller unions abreast of the leading locals. Increasingly uniform conditions, in turn, opened the way to expanded-area bargaining, eventually leading to three basic agreements covering the state. Telephone workers came into the union forces through a series of regional organizations finding their way to a national union and a national contract. Oil workers, who had organized briefly during World War I, renewed their efforts under the National Industrial Recovery Act. Their real breakthrough came after World War II when the union contract finally displaced Standard Oil of California as the wage leader in the industry. The Newspaper Guild won recognition at several major newspapers in the major metropolitan areas and, after a bitter fight, at the *Hollywood Citizen-News*. United Rubber Workers displaced company unions at several major tire plants.

By midcentury, the broad foundations of the state's union movement had been laid. The years ahead would bring changes —major changes in the cases of the farm workers and public employees. But the future directions were clearly marked.

## CHAPTER FOUR

# A Place in the Sun

## Labor in Politics

L ABOR IN POLITICS," observed one political scientist, "is as American as beans and baseball." California workers from the start, as we have seen, frequently turned to government to redress their grievances. Their initial goals—hours of work, wage payments, job safety, workers' compensation—focused on the excesses of the harsh industrial society in which they worked. They utilized their unions, organized central bodies and campaign committees, and, in 1901, formed the California State Federation of Labor to serve their demands on the lawmakers. It was only a short step then to the idea that they help elect the lawmakers. From that realization, debate over tactics in politics has shuttled endlessly from the notion of an independent labor party to Samuel Gompers's dictum: elect labor's friends and defeat its enemies, regardless of party.

Organized labor was under heavy attack in 1916 when the Federation was asked to devise ways of electing candidates pledged "to give labor a greater degree of justice." City central bodies rejected the idea, nine to eight. For a time, it undertook a joint political effort with the Farmers' Union and the Pacific Cooperative League, but it gave up even that limited effort in 1931. California unions, like many other unions across the country, sampled "third party" politics in 1924 when they endorsed the unsuccessful presidential candidacy of Senator Robert M. La Follette. Though he ran well ahead of the Democratic candidate in California, the Federation soon after reaffirmed its traditional form of political activity.

Since 1934, when it endorsed Upton Sinclair, a prominent Socialist writer who captured the Democratic nomination with his depression-inspired program to End Poverty In California (EPIC), labor has been an increasingly active participant in the quadrennial contests for the governor's office. It lost with Sinclair, lost again in 1938 when its candidate in the primary election was defeated by the eventual winner, Culbert Olson. It endorsed Olson four years later but he lost to Earl Warren, later Chief Justice of the United States. It backed Warren in 1946 but turned to James Roosevelt, son of FDR, in 1950 when Warren won a third term. Labor was divided in 1954; the Federation endorsed the Republican candidate and the winner, Goodwin Knight; a group of dissenting unions and their leaders formed a separate committee to work for his opponent.

Labor's endorsement of Edmund G. Brown, Sr., in 1958 was reinforced by his opponent's (Senator William Knowland's) support for Proposition 18 on the ballot, which would have outlawed any form of union security. Aroused and angry, labor staged an intensive, all-out campaign that contributed both to Brown's election and the defeat of the proposition. Brown was challenged in 1962 by Richard M. Nixon, lately an unsuccessful candidate for the presidency. Nixon's antilabor record in the Congress provoked a campaign against him that fell only a little short of labor's intensive 1958 effort. The coalition of Democrats, labor, and minorities failed in 1966, though, when Brown lost to Ronald Reagan, a onetime actor, Democrat, and union official turned conservative Republican. Reagan had no trouble winning a second term over labor's unenthusiastic endorsement of his Democratic opponent, Jesse Unruh. Labor was a prominent and vigorous participant, however, in the 1974 and 1978 races that put Edmund G. Brown, Jr., in the governor's chair.

Organized labor in California (as elsewhere in the United States) took no formal stand in 1932 when Franklin Delano Roosevelt was first elected. Much of it rallied energetically behind him in 1936 and again in 1940 and 1944. The Federation endorsed Harry S. Truman in his successful bid in 1948 and Adlai Stevenson in his unsuccessful races in 1952 and 1956. It threw its weight behind both John F. Kennedy and Lyndon B. Johnson. A last-minute labor drive in 1968 came close to winning California for Senator Hubert Humphrey in the face of Richard Nixon's successful political comeback. Though the AFL-CIO stood aside in 1972, many international unions and much of California labor dug in behind Senator George McGovern. The less-than-enthusiastic support was balanced by labor's dislike of Nixon. Labor mobilized behind Jimmy Carter in 1976, but the state fell to Gerald Ford by less than one percent of the vote.

What most distinguishes these campaigns is the almost straight-line increase in effort and political organization that went into them. If endorsement in the beginning represented little more than a sometimes dubious blessing, labor subsequently invested increasing amounts of time and money in validating its choices. Political action gained importance in labor's eyes after passage in 1947 of the Taft-Hartley amendments to the Wagner Act. They were enacted over President Truman's veto and a surprisingly vigorous and widespread campaign against what labor called a "slave labor" law. The amendments were plainly designed to weaken the protection in the Wagner Act for the workers' right to organize and bargain collectively. In ways both overt and covert, they shifted the balance of power in labor relations, labor felt, toward the employer. In the losses it suffered, labor realized that what government could give, quite plainly government could take away. In 1948, as part of a national pattern, the State Federation established the California Labor League for Political Education. The CIO reinforced its Political Action Committees. As separate entities, the two political groups moved toward support for the same candidates, a similarity in viewpoint that was confirmed by merger in 1958.

Labor's political forces enjoyed the advantage of being able to campaign for an entire slate, extending people and money over a wide range of political contests. Its activities paralleled those of the Democratic Party (with occasional exceptions), leading to collaboration or, at a minimum, side-by-side campaigns. The results were evidenced in the steadily rising number of labor-endorsed, regular party candidates in legislative bodies and public office and, in turn, in an expanding body of labor-sponsored legislation.

Progress on the legislative front had been slow and difficult under Republican state administrations and even in the Democratic Culbert Olson administration, which had been frustrated by Republican control of the legislature. However, the "yellow dog" contract was outlawed at last in 1933. California joined the federal unemployment insurance program in 1935. A law in 1939 created a statewide apprenticeship program. More typical, perhaps, was the Federation report in 1941 on the state senate, among whose forty members it found twenty-three who had not cast a single "good" vote on labor bills.[1]

In the post–World War II sessions of the state legislature, labor has been deeply involved in setting benefit levels, coverage, and other conditions affecting workers' compensation, unemployment insurance, and, since 1946, the disability insurance program covering off-the-job illnesses and accidents. It has been no less concerned with the repeated, insistent attacks on union practices. Nearly every session saw bills aimed at outlawing "hot cargo" (the practice of refusing to handle cargo, freight, or products handled by strikebreakers) and secondary boycotts, or seeking to prohibit any form of union shop or other union security measures. Both types of proposals have also appeared on a number of occasions on the statewide ballot. The scope of labor legislation widened considerably as legislative power was reapportioned, shifting from the rural counties to the metropolitan areas and developing labor-supported Democratic majorities in both houses of the legislature. These developments gave greater range and increased strength to labor endorsements and campaigns. These came into conjunction in the administrations of the Browns, senior and junior. Though interrupted by the two Reagan administrations, labor legislation made long strides forward.

Fair employment practices legislation was enacted. The Brown Act of 1961 and the Meyers-Milias-Brown Act of 1968 opened the way for public employees, for the first time, to organization and to the somewhat elemental form of collective bargaining dubbed "meet-and-confer" (see below). Minimum wage and maximum hours laws that had applied only to women and minors were rewritten to cover men. Rehabilitation was made mandatory under workers' compensation and injured workers were given the right to choose their own doctors, finally dispelling the dictation of "company" doctors. Disability insurance benefits were extended in full to pregnant women workers. Basic collective bargaining and organizational rights were extended initially to farm workers, subsequently to public school employees, employees of the state universities and colleges, and to state employees. Professional strikebreakers were outlawed. Restraints were imposed on the use of injunctions and restraining orders in labor disputes. At the same time, measurable progress was made in bringing benefits levels and other conditions of the social insurance programs up to adequate and equitable levels.[2]

The American workers' habit of "labor in politics" is more than a triumph of union propaganda or union organization. It reflects, imperfectly, a common view of the political world, a product of shared experience and common problems, given crude and uneven expression through the mechanics of democracy. That workers behave differently in the voting booth is strongly suggested in the findings of the California Poll's investigation of voter preference in gubernatorial races from 1959 to 1978.[3] Table 1 underscores the differences in preference for governor voiced by persons in a union family (members of the sample who were union members or whose spouses were members), blue-collar workers, and, in each case, the rest of the sample population.

The differences between the preferences of union families and blue-collar workers and the rest of the poll sample are strong and persistent. Even in 1970, when the union-endorsed

Table 1: Voter Preference for Governor, 1958–1978

| Union-endorsed candidate | Union families | Other families | Blue-collar workers | Other workers |
|---|---|---|---|---|
| 1958 Brown, Sr. | 70.9% | 48.0% | 66.1% | 50.0% |
| 1962 Brown, Sr. | 63.0 | 38.0 | 55.2 | 41.1 |
| 1966 Brown, Sr. | 46.5 | 36.2 | (not available) | |
| 1970 Unruh | 43.7 | 31.8 | 39.7 | 31.9 |
| 1974 Brown, Jr. | 64.9 | 47.5 | 64.6 | 46.0 |
| 1978 Brown, Jr. | 58.5 | 54.4 | 58.1 | 54.6 |

*Source:* California Poll (Field Research Corporation), 1958–1978.

candidate aroused little enthusiasm, the differences in preference are marked. Only in 1978, when consensus was apparently
broader, encouraged by a lackluster opposition candidate, did
the margin narrow; and even then, differences remained. The
data give depth and meaning to the role of "labor in politics."

# Law in the Fields

B Y THE END OF World War I, the shape of California agriculture was increasingly discernible. Concentration of
ownership and operation continued its spread. The number of
one-crop, commercial farms was growing, the number of multi-
crop, "family" farms dwindling. Specialized crops were expanding, some holding or approaching monopolies of the nation's
commercial supplies. Agriculture's appetite for large quantities
of low-cost labor for short, seasonal periods was undiminished.
The work force, taking shape under these circumstances, un-
knowingly faced a half century of bitter, violent struggle for
recognition.

Before the 1920s ended, Carey McWilliams estimated, some
75,000 Mexican workers had joined California's migratory
circle. They were joined over the years by 30,000 Filipino
workers. The Great Depression, for a short time, reversed the
trend. The rate of entry was cut back. Many Mexican workers
voluntarily repatriated themselves while others were repatriated
involuntarily when cities objected to the "relief" burden.[4] For
those who remained, wages dropped sharply: from $1.46 an
hour for chopping an acre of cotton in 1930 to 66 cents in
1932; from $1 a hundred pounds for picking to 40 cents. Field
wages in other crops dropped from 30 cents an hour to $12\frac{1}{2}$
and 15 cents.[5]

A few scattered attempts of Mexican field workers to organize were met with what became characteristic tactics: threats of
deportation, widespread arrests, strikebreakers, and violence,
both threatened and real. Three strikes erupted on California
farms in 1930, three more in the following year, six in 1932;
together they involved about 11,000 workers. In 1933, though,
48,000 workers walked out in thirty-one strikes—half of the

farm strikes in the nation that year and ninety-five percent of the strikers. A few were spontaneous, but they came increasingly under the Communist-led Cannery and Agriculture Workers Union. Two-thirds of the walkouts in 1933 were organized by the CAWIU, involving close to eighty percent of the strikers. About three-fourths of the strikes, according to Stuart Jamieson's study, resulted in wage increases; the rest were broken. None resulted in permanent or continuing organization. The CAWIU itself faded away when the Communist Party abandoned its own "revolutionary" unions in favor of invading mainstream worker organizations.

Growers responded to the outburst of strikes by organizing a new statewide agency, the Associated Farmers. Made up largely of small- and medium-sized farmers, it was "dominated," said *Fortune* magazine, "by the big growers, packers, utilities, banks and other absentee landlords." It demanded prosecution of strike leaders as "traitors" or "subversives" under the state criminal syndicalism law. It campaigned successfully to enact antipicketing ordinances in many counties. It threatened to boycott central cities where unionization impinged on transportation or marketing of agricultural products. Most of all, it raised the casual tactics of violent resistance to unionization to a calculated strategy.

Members pledged to serve in "citizens' armies," though armed with clubs rather than guns. They served as deputies, invading peaceful meetings and crashing picket lines, acting under law enforcement officers, often without the "slightest color of authority." They provided mass escorts for strikebreakers and convoyed growers' trucks. From the Associated Farmers' activities, said the La Follette Committee, "arose the most flagrant and violent infringement of civil liberties." It made virtually a military camp of Salinas in 1936 when an American Federation of Labor union of lettuce packers struck in an effort to renew its contract. The sheriff mobilized the town's able-bodied men into a "citizens' army" under threat of arrest. Under its protection strikebreakers harvested and packed the lettuce. The union was smashed. The Associated Farmers responded the next year with a 1,200-grower army when cannery workers struck in Stockton. The growers' efforts to convoy trucks driven by strikebreakers through the picket lines erupted into violence, tear gas, buck-

shot and rifle bullets injuring at least fifty. "Sheer vigilantism,"
said the La Follette Committee.[6]

Meantime, the character of the farm work force was under-
going drastic change. Drought in the Midwest and Southwest
made refugees of thousands of farmers; dust storms destroyed
their farms and livelihoods. Machinery and large-scale farming in
other areas turned loose more thousands of tenants and share-
croppers. They poured over the Sierra into California—285,000
"in need of manual employment" between 1935 and 1939
were counted by the state's border stations. Sheer numbers
overwhelmed the labor market, flooded labor camps, over-
weighed relief agencies. Destitution, hunger, bewilderment,
and frustration camped with them under bridges, in makeshift
shacks, overcrowded camps, and farm housing. John Steinbeck,
whose *The Grapes of Wrath* captured their travail in fiction,
commented factually: "They are never received into a community nor into the life of a community."[7] For the first time in
generations, California's crops were planted and harvested by a
domestic work force, deridingly dubbed "Okies" and "Arkies."
But the pattern of exploitation changed scarcely at all, nor was
the conflict eased. When the nation went to war in December
1941, thousands of the newcomers were siphoned off into the
armed services and into the shipyards and aircraft plants. Japanese, native- and foreign-born alike, were evacuated and imprisoned. The braceros came to fill their places and for the next
quarter of a century dominated the farm labor market.

In place of unregulated and spontaneous immigration, the
bracero program brought in Mexican nationals under a series of
presidential executive agreements with the Mexican government. It assured growers an adequate number of workers, de-
livered at the right time and right place, and pretty much at the
right price—a program insulated from the general labor market
and virtually union-proof. The braceros came in with guaranteed wages, living conditions, travel, housing, and job opportunities. Wages—low by domestic standards but attractive to jobless Mexican workers—were held under this system pretty
much at 1940 levels throughout the war.

In 1951, Public Law 78 formalized the arrangements that had
developed over the preceding decade. The United States, rather
than the grower, was the contracting party and some conditions

were stiffened. It served to control wages no less effectively. The earnings of over three million Mexican nationals who were employed in 275 important crop areas between 1950 and 1960 were held virtually steady—an average of $1,680 in 1950, $1,666 in 1959, by Ernesto Galarza's estimate. (Factory workers' weekly earnings in the same period increased by sixty percent—on an annual basis, from $3,400 to $5,423.) The advantages of a closely controlled labor pool, regulated by a flexible, virtually unlimited supply of braceros, were never better demonstrated. It made all the more understandable the growers' anguished cries when Public Law 78 was allowed to expire in December 1964.

Nearly a year later, grape pickers in Delano went on strike.[9] They were members of the Agricultural Workers Organizing Committee (AWOC), remnant of an earlier AFL-CIO organizing attempt. They were joined ten days later by members of the National Farm Workers Association (NFWA). The AWOC, mainly Filipino, came from a union background, while the NFWA, Mexican and Spanish-speaking, came from a community-organization orientation. One looked to the union movement for support; the other drew backing in greater measure from church, civil rights, and student groups. It was a difficult, often awkward and uneasy alliance, but it launched what proved to be a fifteen-year war to build a lasting union of farm workers.

After a long and bitter winter, it greeted spring with a twenty-four-day, three-hundred-mile march from Delano to the steps of the capitol in Sacramento, capping it with word that Schenley Industries would recognize the unions and the giant DiGiorgio Corporation would agree to worker elections to determine representation. The alliance signed its first contract, embodying full union recognition and a 35-cents-an-hour wage increase, with Schenley on June 21. To contest the DiGiorgio elections, the two organizations came together in the AFL-CIO-sponsored United Farm Workers Organizing Committee (later chartered as the AFL-CIO United Farm Workers of America). Field workers chose the AFL-CIO group in preference to the Teamsters; other workers and truck drivers chose the latter. Arbitration finally settled the second major, but short-lived, contract; it was lost three years later when the DiGiorgio properties were sold.

The table grape growers in Delano were joined in their hold-out against the union by those in the southern growing areas. Backed by the AFL-CIO, the UFWOC launched a boycott of table grapes that eventually extended across the continent and overseas. The breakthrough came in the spring of 1970 when growers in the Coachella Valley signed with the union; the Delano growers soon followed suit. "This is the beginning of a new day," said César Chávez, the charismatic leader of the farm workers. Said AFL-CIO president George Meany, formally ending the grape boycott. "Unionization has moved to the point where we can see the end of the road."

The farm workers' momentum carried them, almost without pause, into the lettuce fields of the Salinas and Santa Maria areas and into still another confrontation with the Teamsters. To head off the Chávez push, the growers hastily recognized the Teamsters, though they delayed writing the actual contracts until later. Angry lettuce workers began leaving the fields. A truce between the rival unions was hastily pasted together, reiterating a 1967 treaty that had recognized UFWOC in the fields, the Teamsters in the sheds and on the trucks. The 1970 version, however, gave growers the option of keeping their Teamster contracts; and overwhelmingly they did. Chávez called for a strike, and thousands responded. The growers asked the courts to outlaw the strikes, claiming they were caught in a jurisdictional battle between rival unions. With a single exception, the courts willingly complied. The strike gave way, then, to a lettuce boycott, cut over the same pattern as the earlier, successful grape boycott. The farm workers dug in for a long struggle.

The farm workers' insistent drive was countered in 1972 with a grower-sponsored ballot proposition, No. 22, that would have imposed rigid, one-sided restrictions on farm workers' rights to organize or negotiate, to conduct strikes or boycotts. The union mobilized farm workers and recruited widespread union and community backing in an intensive "vote no" campaign. The proposition was defeated, 4.6 million votes to 3.3 million. The growers lost another battle soon after when the California Supreme Court overturned the injunctions that had halted the 1970 lettuce strike. The growers had designated the Teamsters as the farm workers' bargaining agent, the court said, though they must have known that the Teamsters did not represent the workers. It would not, the court ruled, put the power of the state behind the growers' choice. But it did not overturn the Teamster contracts.

The Teamsters soon began renegotiating their lettuce and vegetable agreements, but with an eye cocked on the UFWOC grape contracts expiring in 1973. When the UFW's efforts to renew its Coachella Valley grape agreements ran into a dead end, the growers quickly signed the Teamsters' more generous offers, embodying several concessions ardently desired by the growers but refused by the UFW. AFL-CIO president Meany labeled it "disgraceful union-busting." It provoked a running, five-month fight. Two UFW members were killed and hundreds injured when Teamster "guards" and organizers charged UFW picket lines with tire chains and baseball bats and attacked UFW supporters. The fight moved to the Delano area. Courts ordered the strikes halted, but thousands of UFW pickets and supporters went to jail for refusing to obey the injunctions. Even while high-level attempts were renewed to negotiate another AFL-CIO-Teamster truce, the Delano growers signed Teamster contracts. When the harvest was done, the UFW was left with only a handful of contracts, covering 6,500 workers; a year before the UFW had held 150 contracts covering 50,000 workers. Meantime, Teamsters president Frank Fitzsimmons scuttled a new proposal to end the interunion warfare. The Teamsters intervention was widely interpreted as a "sweetheart" arrangement with notable advantages for the growers and Teamsters, and little, if any, benefit for the farm workers. "The time-tested and time-honored code of morality in the trade union movement," Meany said, "has been that the strong help the weak, not that the strong destroy the weak."

Taking office as governor in January 1975, Edmund G. Brown, Jr., gave high priority to enactment of a farm labor relations law. His administration's proposal drew objections from virtually everyone concerned, but the governor successfully reconciled the differences. He signed the bill into law on June 5.

The new law declared the right of farm workers to bargain collectively through representatives of their own choosing—a declaration without precedent in agricultural labor relations in either state or federal law. It had been withheld from farm workers forty-two years earlier when it had been granted to industrial workers in the National Industrial Recovery Act; no state before had ever affirmed it. Its denial could in overwhelming part be held responsible for the conflict, the violence, and the exploitation that had burdened the farm worker over the years. The law provided secret-ballot elections to allow farm workers to choose or reject bargaining representatives, the only way union recognition could lawfully be won. It affirmed the right of farm workers (once recognized) to strike or to boycott, both direct and secondary, in seeking a union contract. Existing agreements (such as the Teamsters') remained in force but could not be renewed without giving the workers an opportunity to reject or affirm the responsible union. It created a five-member Agricultural Labor Relations Board to administer the law, conduct union representation elections, and adjudge allegations of unfair labor practices. It set time limits in which elections must be held, both to minimize interference with farm operations and to keep abreast of the workers' migrations.

Trouble was clearly ahead, though, when the new board went to work in August 1975. It adopted an access rule which allowed organizers to enter an employer's property to solicit support, with limits on time, place, and number of organizers. The rule drew angry fire, and like the act itself, was quickly challenged in court. Nevertheless, the board held its first election in September; 194 elections followed in the first month. The board was assaulted with charges of inexperience, inefficiency, and bias, but its budget finally tripped it up. It had started with a $1.3 million appropriation which quickly ran out under the heavy caseload. The board borrowed another $1.25 million from the State Emergency Fund, but the legislature refused to vote a deficiency appropriation. The board was forced finally to halt operations on April 2, warehouse its records, and close its offices. The board appropriation for the upcoming year was held hostage to angry demands to abolish the access rule and to protests against board "bias" raised by growers and Teamsters. The dispute war was finally resolved by creating an "oversight" committee; a $6.7 million budget was approved and the ALRB, now largely reconstituted, returned to work.

The roadblocks to the appropriation had been cleared in good part by an initiative measure put on the ballot by the UFW. Proposition 14 would have reenacted the Agricultural Labor Relations Act, but the access provision had been stiffened, a more generous provision was made for providing the union with lists of employees, and the law toughened in other ways. Growers decided they preferred the existing law to the new UFW version. After the new appropriation had been approved, Proposition 14 went down to defeat.

The UFW and the Teamsters signed a new peace treaty in March 1977. In effect, it affirmed earlier, though disavowed, agreements on jurisdiction: the field workers for the UFW, the packing-shed workers and truck drivers for the Teamsters. The Teamsters also agreed they would not renew contracts currently held in the UFW area; they also withdrew from all elections and related matters pending before the ALRB.

By then, the UFW had piled up a substantial lead in ALRB voting. The UFW won majorities in 229 elections in the ALRB's first year—76 where more than one union was on the ballot. The Teamsters won 116—71 in contested votes. The UFW's popular vote doubled that for the Teamsters.

The law cleared the way to recognition and collective bargaining, but it has by no means achieved its goal of "peace in the agricultural fields." When the UFW sought in 1979 to renew contracts covering some 7,000 workers and to obtain a substantial wage increase, the growers fought back in customary style. Farm guards, said a UFW spokesman, "were armed to the teeth with pistols, shotguns and clubs and sent in to provoke violence and revive racial antagonism that has long existed in the Imperial Valley." When a UFW member was killed, an Imperial County judge ordered grower guards disarmed and kept apart from UFW pickets. But the battle raged through the harvest season and continued deep into the 1980 season. Slowly, though, the UFW increased its roster of signed agreements and, by thousands, the number of its members covered by them. The rules had been changed but the struggle went on.

# Begging and Bargaining

B EFORE 1966, California had never experienced a teachers' strike. "And not until 1969," a study added, "were there significant strikes" among public employees.[10] The time for strikes and for collective bargaining in the public sector arrived in the 1970s.[11]

In the George Brown Act of 1961, the legislature wrote into law the right of public employees to join organizations and the duty of public agencies to "meet and confer" with their representatives. Beyond that, it obligated public agencies only to "consider" the presentations of employee organizations. Final decisions were left, beyond challenge, in the hands of the agencies' governing bodies. It made no serious dent in existing practice. Employees had usually been free to make presentations through their organizations to local governing bodies. Their presentations may have been accompanied by lobbying or informal consultation, a process early public employee unionists labeled "collective begging."

Public employees walked out on strike in a number of jurisdictions in the mid-1960s. The city of Anaheim recognized a service employees union as bargaining agent for the employees of its stadium and convention center. Ventura County by 1967 had written a detailed employee relations policy which required "good faith" conferences; it also devised a procedure for formal recognition of employee organizations. Marin County and, in even greater detail, Los Angeles County devised formal structures for collective bargaining.

The George Brown Act gave way in 1968 to the Meyers-Milias-Brown Act. The law now called on public employers to "meet and confer" with representatives of recognized employee organizations under a "mutual obligation" to "endeavor to reach agreement." The resulting agreement was required to be framed in a nonbinding memorandum of understanding for submission to the governing body. Probably the act's greatest virtue was to allow public agencies, within loose guidelines, to adopt their own rules governing employer-employee relations after "consultation in good faith" with representatives of their employees. Local jurisdictions were free to fill in the blanks in the act, which omitted such practical matters as bargaining units, recognition procedures, representation elections, unfair labor practices, impasse procedures, and work stoppages. It set no penalties for noncompliance, nor did it create administrative machinery.

The act left little doubt, however, that final decision rested, not in the bargaining or "meet-and-confer" process, but in the governing bodies of the public agencies. Nothing in the act, it said, "shall be deemed to supersede the provisions of existing rules of local public agencies which provide for a merit or civil service system." It was intended "to strengthen merit, civil service, and other methods of administering employer-employee relations through the establishment of uniform and orderly methods of communications between employees and public agencies."

The new measure left public employee relations law in a state described in the 1971 study as "primitive." The act covered city, county, and special district employees only loosely; effective implementation was left largely in local hands. Public school employees were ineffectively covered by the Winton Act (about which, more shortly). Transit district workers were frequently covered by labor relations policies laid down in the separate basic laws creating the districts. State employees had the fewest rights of all. Rights and duties of employees, employee organizations, and public employers were confused and contradictory. The process of resolving the contradictions and ending the confusion was left to local government, sometimes to employee organizations, and, as always, to the courts.

The changing law was both an incentive and a response to employee organization. While the number of government employees in California had risen 475 percent between 1950 and 1977, the number of state and local public workers in unions multiplied 730 percent. The proportion of government employees (federal as well as state and local) in unions rose from 12 to 18 percent and the proportion of government workers in the state's union movement climbed from 5 to 14 percent. As more and more local jurisdictions granted exclusive bargaining rights to majority unions, an increasing number of formerly local, independent associations moved into union affiliation, thus speeding union growth. The process frequently ended costly, often bitter and wasteful competition for exclusive bargaining status; it brought the association members the benefit of collective bargaining skills and the often-influential legislative experience of private-sector unions, as well as wide-based local, state, and national support of the union movement.

Local governments and employee organizations struggled to

put the act's loose guidelines to work, producing in the process a varying assortment of employment relations patterns. The law's uncertainties were sometimes in the background of the sharply increased number of public sector strikes that erupted, especially in the latter half of the 1970s. Inexperience among employee organizations and public employers contributed to the conflict, as did the struggle of local governing bodies to reconcile employee demands with tax revenues. In 1978, the heightened, often angry and vindictive tax consciousness aroused by the Jarvis-Gann amendment, Proposition 13, created strong and insistent pressures, exacerbated by the coincidence of rising living costs. Conflicts arose, too, over noneconomic issues that assumed major importance, such as binding arbitration of grievances, workloads, job security, and various forms of union security.

In 1966, according to the California Division of Labor Statistics, 5,800 public employees were involved in eighteen strikes at a cost of 27,500 person-days of work. The average strike lasted five days. In 1974, 37,300 public employees gave up 409,400 person-days of work. In 1979 those days of idleness soared to 513,000, involving 36,700 employees. The duration of the average strike climbed from 11 days in 1974 to 23 days in 1976, but then dropped back to 14 in 1979.

From 1974, the *California Public Employee Relations Magazine* reported, public schools and local government experienced nearly identical numbers of strikes. In 1975, public schools accounted for only a quarter of public employee strikes. The upsurge reflected the changing structure of public school employee relations. They had been covered by the feeble strictures of the George Brown Act until superseded in 1965 by the Winton Act. The new law created a form of proportional representation of teacher organizations on a "certified staff council." The act called on school management to "meet and confer . . . in a conscientious effort to reach agreement." But the obligation was imposed lightly and the final decision in any case remained in the hands of the school board. The act was strongly influenced by the California Teachers' Association's effort to blanket the smaller unions affiliated with the AFL-CIO American Federation of Teachers. The councils often seemed more effective in creating disunity among teacher organizations than in their negotiating functions. Growing pressure from the teachers' unions and, in the background, from the union movement brought the CTA closer to union-like behavior. Its goals moved perceptibly closer to those of the teachers' union. It recognized the right of its members to strike. It sought legal sanction for enforceable agreements, binding arbitration of grievances, exclusive bargaining status (though by membership count, rather than by secret-ballot elections).

A long and major step toward a more advanced structure of employee relations in the schools was taken in the Rodda Act of 1976. Modeled far more closely after the National Labor Relations Act for private industry, it created a three-member Educational Employment Relations Board (EERB) and gave it the job of administering the law. It fell to the EERB to determine bargaining units, conduct representation elections, judge and correct unfair labor practices, and invoke the impasse procedures provided by the law in deadlocked negotiations. Within its first year, the EERB estimated, four-fifths of the state's 1,170 school districts were involved in implementing the law.

The legislature in 1977 extended collective bargaining procedures and guarantees to the state's civil service employees. Formed in the same general mold as the Rodda Act, the new law was also to be administered by the EERB, now renamed the Public Employment Relations Board (PERB). In 1978, substantially similar rights and procedures were extended to employees of the Hastings College of Law, the University of California, and the California State University and Colleges system. This law, too, is similar to the earlier legislation and is also administered by the PERB.

Meantime collective bargaining in local government was only as effective as local ordinances and administration allowed it to be. The degree of effectiveness ranged as a result from the totally absent to broad-gauged, fully implemented structures embracing practices and principles of collective bargaining developed in private industry. Increasingly those precedents—generated in nearly half a century under the National Labor Relations Act and its administrative agency, the National Labor Relations Board—are becoming the guidelines for public employee relations as well. Local government employment relations, however, are still dogged by the reservations underlying

the Meyer-Milias-Brown Act: the absence of uniform standards
and procedures, but most of all, its declared intent not to supersede but to strengthen locally governed merit or civil service
systems. The final decisions, the law said, remain with the
governing bodies of the public agencies. Whether the unilateral
decision-making of the one system and of government itself can
be accommodated to the bilateral mechanics of collective bargaining is one of two overriding issues confronting workers,
management, and public officials in local government. The second issue involves the question of whether an adequate and
equitable substitute can be found for the strike. Some areas of
government involve critical services where work stoppages are
considered unacceptable by many sections of the public. Nevertheless, experience shows plainly that strikes do occur in those
areas. Collective bargaining in the public sector will be shaped
in the years ahead by developing answers to these questions.

# Labor's Role

B ETWEEN 1950 AND 1977, California added 5.2 million
workers to its payrolls and another half million to its unemployment rolls. The massive increase more than doubled the
1950 work force, accenting the changing contours of the state's
economy and reflecting the drift, apparent at least since midcentury, to a predominantly white-collar work force. These
developments, in turn, left their mark on the state's unions.

About two-thirds of the newcomers took white-collar jobs;
about one-sixth went into service trades, slightly more than a
fifth into blue-collar occupations. Where white-collar workers
in 1950 made up 45 percent of the work force, they rose to 56
percent in 1977; the blue-collar segment dropped from 36
percent to 29; the service element rose from 12 percent to 13;
and the farm work force fell from about 6 percent to 2. Table 2
shows the changes that took place in the work force and in the
union movement in those years.

While the work force gained 5,310,000 recruits, only 790,000
of them joined unions. The union sector of the wage-and-salary
work force, as a result, fell from 43 to 25 percent. Such meas-

Table 2: Increases in Wage-and-Salary Work Force (Non-Farm)
and Union Membership, 1950 to 1977

| | Wage-and-salary work force | | Union membership | |
|---|---|---|---|---|
| | Number* | Percent | Number* | Percent |
| Total | 5,310 | 167 | 789.6 | 59 |
| Service industries | 1,679 | 300 | 74.2 | 32 |
| Government | 1,201 | 225 | 244.5 | 378 |
| Trade | 1,187 | 152 | 174.7 | 142 |
| Manufacturing | 950 | 125 | 123.5 | 28 |
| Transport/public utilities | 167 | 55 | 90.9 | 40 |
| Construction | 126 | 53 | 81.8 | 33 |
| *In thousands | | | | |

Source: Calculated from data of the California Division of Labor Statistics and Research.

ures of union penetration, though, tend to misstate the strategic position of the unions. The relative numbers would be higher, of course, if "workers" were eliminated who are not in any practical sense potential union members: corporation presidents, for example, and management at nearly every level, employees of small firms, and rural workers in whatever industry. The numbers increase, too, as they focus more sharply on industries traditionally rooted in manual labor where unions historically have grown. The big gains in jobs, on the other hand, have come in recent times in largely nonmanual occupations—in trade, service industries, government—and in econonic areas increasingly distant from the historical sources of union strength. The development poses a serious challenge to labor's economic strength and to its influence beyond the bargaining table, both of which until now derived from its penetration of strategic economic sectors.

Organization of workers in the developing sectors of the work force faces formidable obstacles. The "ripple" effect of union standards pushes employers to improve conditions in an effort, often successful, to remain "union-free." Minimum-wage and maximum-hour standards, low or evaded as they sometimes are, still plant barriers to gross exploitation of workers and reduce the incentive to join unions. Short-term employment, part-time jobs, lower requirements for many entry-level jobs, and high turnover increasingly characterize the new jobs, especially in retail and service industries. The impulse to self-organization that fueled the great upsurge of unionism in the 1930s for now seems stilled. The union movement has been slow or unwilling or unable to undertake large-scale organizing efforts in many difficult or inaccessible areas of the economy.

The chief obstacle to organization, however, has been the persistent, historical opposition of employers, singly and in legions, to unions of their employees. Its more blatant forms have been tamed by labor relations legislation, but it survives in good health. It may be unlawful to fire or refuse to hire an employee for joining or supporting a union, but sophisticated psychological testing and so-called "lie detectors" provide more subtle, alternative screening devices. Nationally known firms of lawyers and labor relations consultants have built a "growth" industry on antiunionism. Seminars and publications instruct employers on how to defeat organizing campaigns, avoid union agreements, and get rid of unions in their workplaces. They provide determined employers with tailored campaigns or with legal counsel on how to exploit every gap and every delay in the law in order to oppose unions and defeat collective bargaining. Efforts to cure these defects in the nation's labor laws ran aground on a massive shoal of employer opposition.

Traditional antiunion organizations of employers still do business, though behind refurbished fronts. California unionists faced (and defeated) a frontal attack in 1958 in the so-called "right to work" ballot proposition. Restrictions on the rights of public employee organizations frequently appear on local ballots. Perhaps more significant is the rise of corporate political action committees (named, ironically, after the political wing of the former CIO). In California's 1978 general election, political action committees, organized and financed by corporate managements and their allies, poured over $15 million into state and local political contests, more than $10 for every dollar contributed by employee organizations. Such lopsided campaign financing must inevitably force its influence on state and local lawmakers. A dozen or more bills in the 1978 legislature, for example, sought to weaken key sections of the Agricultural Labor Relations Act. Other measures proposed outright prohibition of public employee strikes. More—over a broader range—can be expected.

Not the least of the barriers confronting unions is an atmosphere that varies from indifferent to hostile. The Field Institute found, in a 1977 poll, that "a majority of people (56%) believe that unions 'do more good than harm' but a substantial number (28%) feels that they have a more harmful than beneficial effect."[12] Asked what they think is good about unions, people most often named higher wages and living conditions, safer working conditions, "protection for workers"—all more or less readily verifiable. Asked to name "bad things" about unions, they replied in terms that, as generalizations, are simply unverifiable or even untrue: "too powerful, too strong"; "promotes unnecessary strikes"; "union leaders are corrupt." Their replies, indeed, echo the very aspects of the unions that have received by far the major attention of the media, both print and broadcast. If they are true in individual cases, it is demonstrably wrong to apply the labels to the nearly three million union members in California, to their unions or their leaders. Nevertheless, the media-induced climate supplies a comfortable environment for the union-busters and ready-made rationalizations for open-shop employers.

Hostility also leans heavily on suspicions that, somehow, unions and their officials do not represent—or misrepresent— their members. The same Field Institute study asked union members in its sample about their degree of commitment "to the labor movement as a whole." A majority (55%) said it was either "very strongly" or "moderately strongly" committed; "many" (43%), the study said, are "rather non-committal." But the study gives no intimation of what any degree of commitment actually meant in concrete terms or how it translated into the union members' specific responses to their unions. The study did learn that "about one in three union members acknowledged that they vote for union-recommended candidates," but a sizable proportion "often" disagree with state of national union leaders. These findings have been frequently contradicted—the study referred to earlier showed significant contrasts—but the more important point is that these questions (and their almost predictable results) again echo the suspicions and underlying hostility of the media atmosphere. Nor does it end there: an examination of curricula in secondary schools and higher education quickly reveals that labor's role in the society is understated where it is not largely ignored. A good many unionists feel strongly that unions generally and workers particularly are underrepresented or grossly caricatured in television and movies as well as in the print and broadcast media.

These grievances are, perhaps, the inevitable result of labor's role in society: often challenging accepted values and established leadership at important intersections; working at the cutting edge of public policy where dissent is often unpopular and unwelcome; speaking for large sections of the work force (and the general population), union members or not, who have no other voice in public decisions; contradicting established sentiment and conventional wisdom. The distance between the union movement and conventional wisdom varies widely; it is wider—or narrower—at some times than others. Neither scorn, nor distaste, nor rejection, however, stems its ultimate conviction that it is entitled to occupy its place in the sun. That, in essence, has been its history.

# NOTES

## CHAPTER ONE

1. S. F. Cook, "The Conflict between the California Indian and White Civilization," *Ibero-Americana*, XXI (1943), 91–101.

2. Quoted in Oscar Lewis, *San Francisco: Mission to Metropolis* (Berkeley: Howell-North, 1966), 14.

3. Zoeth Skinner Eldredge, *The Beginnings of San Francisco* (San Francisco: Eldredge, 1912), 155.

4. Quoted in Carey McWilliams, *California: The Great Exception* (1949; Santa Barbara, Calif.: Peregrine Smith, 1976), 52.

5. S. F. Cook, *The Population of the California Indians, 1769–1970* (Berkeley: University of California Press, 1976), 42–65.

6. Guillermo Prieto, *San Francisco in the Seventies* (San Francisco: John Henry Nash, 1938), 15.

7. John Walton Caughey, *Gold Is the Cornersone* (Berkeley: University of California Press, 1948), 224.

8. Frank Soulé, John H. Gihon, and James Nisbet, *The Annals of San Francisco* (New York: D. Appleton, 1855), 202.

9. Quoted in Joseph Henry Jackson, ed., *The Western Gate: A San Francisco Reader* (New York: Farrar, Straus & Young, 1952), 150.

10. Ira B. Cross, *A History of the Labor Movement in California* (Berkeley: University of California Press, 1935), 19–28.

11. Quoted in Roger W. Lotchin, *San Francisco, 1846–1856: From Hamlet to City* (New York: Oxford University Press, 1975), 84.

12. See, among others, John Walton Caughey, *California* (3rd ed., Englewood Cliffs, N.J.: Prentice-Hall, 1970); Lewis, *San Francisco;* Alexander Saxton, *The Indispensable Enemy: Labor and the Anti-Chinese Movement* (Berkeley: University of California Press, 1971); Cross, *History of the Labor Movement,* chap. 4.

13. California Statutes, 1867–1868, 63.

14. Lucille Eaves, *A History of California Labor Legislation* (Berkeley: University of California Press, 1910), 207.

## CHAPTER TWO

1. Quoted in Ira B. Cross, *A History of the Labor Movement in California* (Berkeley: University of California Press, 1935), 63.

2. Quoted in Neil Larry Shumsky, "Tar Flat and Nob Hill: A Social History of Industrial San Francisco during the 1870s" (Ph.D. dissertation, University of California, Berkeley, 1972), 113.

3. Neil L. Shumsky, ed., "Frank Roney's San Francisco—His Diary: April 1875–March 1876," *Labor History,* XVII (1976), 246.

4. Shumsky, "Tar Flat and Nob Hill," 13.

5. Alexander Saxton, *The Indispensable Enemy: Labor and the Anti-Chinese Movement* (Berkeley: University of California Press, 1971), 16.

6. Carey McWilliams, *California: The Great Exception* (1949; Santa Barbara, Calif.: Peregrine Smith, 1976), 52.

7. Saxton, *Indispensable Enemy,* 112.

8. Quoted in Henry George, "The Kearney Agitation in California," *Popular Science Monthly,* XVII (August 1880), 433.

9. Statistics dealing with population, labor force, manufacturing employment and earnings have been drawn from the reports of the U.S. Bureau of the Census in its present and earlier incarnations.

10. Quoted in Paul Taylor and Norman Leon Gold, "San Francisco and the General Strike," *Survey Graphic,* XXIII (September 1934), 405.

11. The narrative of the 1901 teamsters and waterfront strikes has been drawn in substantial part from Bernard Cornelius Cronin, *Father Yorke and the Labor Movement in San Francisco, 1900–1910* (Washington, D.C.: Catholic University of America Press, 1943), 39–89; Ira B. Cross, "California Labor Notes" (manuscript, Bancroft Library, University of California, Berkeley), folder 24, 1901–1902; Thomas Walker Page, "The San Francisco Labor Movement in 1901," *Political Science Quarterly,* XVII (December 1902), 672–687; Robert M. Robinson, "San Francisco Teamsters at the Turn of the Century," *California Historical Society Quarterly,* XXXV 1935), 145; Robert E. L. Knight, *Industrial Relations in the San Francisco Bay Area, 1900–1918* (Berkeley: University of California Press, 1960), 62–98.

12. Knight, *Industrial Relations,* 86.

13. Ray Stannard Baker, "A Test of Men," *American Magazine,* November 1906, 81.

14. Principal sources for this section are Lucille Eaves, *A History of California Labor Legislation* (Berkeley: University of California Press, 1910); Cross, *History of the Labor Movement;* Earl G. Crockett, "The History of California Labor Legislation, 1910–1930" (Ph.D. dissertation, University of California, Berkeley, 1931); Paul Scharrenberg, "California State Federation of Labor: A History Covering the First Half of the Century, 1901–1950" (undated manuscript in author's possession).

15. An open shop theoretically is open to union members and non-members alike without discrimination. In practice it usually bars union members, since its intent is to frustrate the increased economic strength of workers acting in concert, which is the essence of union. The result invariably is the emasculation or destruction of collective bargaining. The open shop, said Mr. Dooley (a humorous commentator in the early years of this century), "'tis where they kape the doors open to accommodate th' constant stream av min comin' in t'take jobs cheaper than th' min what has the jobs." The open shop, Dooley added, has no objections to "properly conducted" unions: "No strikes, no rules, no contracts, no scales, hardly iny wages, an' damn few members."

16. This section, climaxed by the *Los Angeles Times* bombing, is drawn mainly from Grace Heilman Stimson, *Rise of the Labor Movement in Los Angeles* (Berkeley: University of California Press, 1955); Carey McWilliams, *Southern California Country: An Island on the Land* (New York: Duell, Sloan & Pearce, 1946), 118–283; Cross, *History of the Labor Movement,* particularly chap. 14; Knight, *Industrial Relations,* 226–235; Robert Glass Cleland, *California in Our Time (1900–1940)* (New York: Knopf, 1947), 74–87; Louis B. and Richard S. Perry, *A History of the Los Angeles Labor Movement, 1911–1941* (Los Angeles: Institute of Industrial Relations, University of California, 1963), chap. 1; and "Story of Forty-Year War for Free City," *Los Angeles Times,* October 1–November 2, 1929.

17. John A. Fitch, "Los Angeles, A Militant Anti-Union Citadel," *The Survey,* XXXI (March 21, 1914), 768.

18. Quoted in Carey McWilliams, *Factories in the Fields* (Boston: Little Brown, 1939), 22.

19. Carleton H. Parker, *The Casual Laborer and Other Essays* (New York: Harcourt, Brace & Howe, 1920), 61.

20. The account of the Wheatland riots draws heavily on Carleton Parker's initial report, published as an appendix to *The Casual Laborer;* "The California Casual and His Revolt," *Quarterly Journal of Economics,* XXX (November 1915), 110; and "The Wheatland Riot and What Lay

Back of It," *The Survey,* XXXI (March 21, 1914), 768; the "Wheatland Scrapbooks" in the Bancroft Library, University of California, Berkeley; Stuart Jamieson, "Labor Unionism in Agriculture," U.S. Dept. of Labor, Bureau of Labor Statistics, *Bulletin No. 836* (Washington, D.C., 1945); George L. Bell, "The Wheatland Hop-Field Riot," *Outlook,* CVII (May 16, 1914), 118.

21. The narrative of these years draws from San Francisco Chamber of Commerce, "Law and Order in San Francisco: A Beginning" (1916) (Bancroft Library, University of California, Berkeley); Knight, *Industrial Relations;* Cleland, *California in Our Time,* 94–100; Harry F. Grady, "The Open Shop in San Francisco," *The Survey,* XXXVII (November 25, 1916), 192; William Martin Camp, *San Francisco: Port of Gold* (New York: Doubleday, 1948), 315–427; Curt Gentry, *Frame-up* (New York: W. W. Norton, 1967).

22. See Frederick Lynne Ryan, "Industrial Relations in the San Francisco Building Trades" (Ph.D. dissertation, University of California, Berkeley, 1930); Paul Eliel, "San Francisco, A Free City,"*Law and Labor,* XII (March–April 1930), 53, 83.

23. David Warren Ryder, "The Unions Lose San Francisco," *American Mercury,* VII (April 1926), 412.

## CHAPTER THREE

1. Irving Bernstein, "Unemployment in the Great Depression," in *The Second Welfare Forum* (New York: Columbia University Press, 1959), 39.

2. For reports on the waterfront and general strike, see Mike Quin, *The Big Strike* (Olema, Calif.: Olema Publishing Co., 1949); Paul Eliel, *The Waterfront and General Strikes: San Francisco, 1934* (San Francisco: Industrial Association of San Francico, 1934); Ira B. Cross, *A History of the Labor Movement in California* (Berkeley: University of California Press 1935); 254–262; *Waterfront Worker,* February 1933– May 1934; Paul Taylor and Leon Gold, "San Francisco and the General Strike," *Survey Graphic,* XXIII (September 1934), 405. In addition, the following documents in the Bancroft Library, University of California, Berkeley, have been used: Thomas G. Plant, "Statement to the National Longshoremen's Board, July 11, 1934" (Waterfront Employers Union of San Francisco, 1934); George P. Hedley, "The Strike as I Have Seen It," an address before the Church Council for Social Education, Berkeley, California, July 19, 1934; Herman Phleger, "Oral Argument in Behalf of Waterfront Employers Before the National Longshoremen's Board," September 25, 1934; and transcripts of proceedings before the National Longshoremen's Board, July and September, 1934.

3. Louis B. and Richard S. Perry, *A History of the Los Angeles Labor Movement, 1911–1941* (Los Angeles: Institute of Industrial Relations, University of California, 1963), viii.

4. The union membership figures are drawn from the California Division of Labor Statistics and Research, *Union Labor in California,* which initiated an annual census in 1950.

5. Clark Kerr, "Collective Bargaining on the Pacific Coast,"*Monthly Labor Review,* LXIV (April 1947), 650.

6. Gordon W. Bertram and Sherman J. Maisel, *Industrial Relations in the Construction Industry: The Northern California Experience* (Berkeley: Institute of Industrial Relations, University of California, 1956).

7. Betty V. H. Schneider and Abraham Siegel, *Industrial Relations in the Pacific Coast Longshore Industry* (Berkeley: Institute of Industrial Relations, University of California, 1956).

8. Lincoln Fairley, *Facing Mechanization: The West Coast Longshore Plan* (Los Angeles: Institute of Industrial Relations, University of California, 1979).

9. Arthur P. Allen and Betty V. H. Schneider *Industrial Relations in the California Aircraft Industry* (Berkeley: Institute of Industrial Relations, University of California, 1956).

10. Hugh Lovell and Tasile Carter, *Collective Bargaining in the Motion Picture Industry* (Berkeley: Institute of Industrial Relations, University of California, 1955).

## CHAPTER FOUR

1. Paul Scharrenberg, "California State Federation of Labor: A History Covering the First Half of the Century, 1901–1950" (undated manuscript in author's possession).

2. Drawn from the annual legislative reviews published by the California Labor Federation, AFL-CIO.

3. Data for this study, originally collected by the Field Research Corporation, were provided by the University of California Data Program, Berkeley. These organizations are not responsible for the analysis and interpretation of data appearing here.

4. Carey McWilliams, *Factories in the Fields* (Boston: Little, Brown, 1939), 124.

5. Stuart Jamieson, "Labor Unionism in Agriculture," U.S. Dept. of Labor, Bureau of Labor Statistics, *Bulletin No. 836* (Washington, D.C., 1945), 100.

6. See various hearings and reports of the U.S. Congress, Senate, Committee on Education and Labor, "Violations of the Right of Free Speech and Assembly...," *Hearings,* 76th, 77th, and 78th Congresses (1940–1944).

7. John Steinbeck, *Their Blood Is Strong* (San Francisco: Simon J. Lubin Society, 1938).

8. Ernesto Galarza, *Merchants of Labor: The Mexican Bracero Story* (San Jose, Calif.: published by the author, 1964), 135.

9. For the account that follows I have drawn from, among many, Peter Matthiessen, *Sal Si Puedes* (New York: Random House, 1969); Jacques Levy, *César Chávez: Autobiography of La Causa* (New York: Norton, 1975); Dick Meister and Anne Loftis, *A Long Time Coming: The Struggle to Unionize America's Farm Workers* (New York: Macmillan, 1977); *Northern California Labor,* 1964 to date; California Agricultural Labor Relations Board, *First Annual Report, 1976 and 1977* (Sacramento: 1978).

10. David Bowen, Peter Feuille, and George Strauss, "The California Experience," in *Unionization of Municipal Employees: Proceedings of the Academy of Political Science* XXX (December 1970), 107.

11. The development of collective bargaining by public employees is chronicled in some detail in *California Public Employee Relations,* a publication of the Institute of Industrial Relations, University of California, Berkeley, 1969 to date.

12. Data for this study, originally collected by the Field Research Corporation, were provided by the University of California Data Program, Berkeley. These organizations are not responsible for the analysis and interpretation of data appearing here.

# SUGGESTED READINGS

I RA B. CROSS laid the essential foundation in his invaluable
*A History of the Labor Movement in California* (Berkeley: University of California Press, 1935). Its comprehensive coverage of the nineteenth-century beginnings of the labor movement has not been equaled. His "California Labor Notes" (in the Bancroft Library, University of California, Berkeley) supply an abundance of added detail. Lucille Eaves in *A History of California Labor Legislation* (Berkeley: University of California Press, 1910) traces the roots of protective laws from the state's beginnings to 1910. Earl C. Crockett's "The History of California Labor Legislation" (Ph.D. dissertation, University of California, Berkeley, 1931) continued the coverage in much the same fashion to 1930.

Several regional histories pick up the general labor story: Grace Heilman Stimson covered the early years in Los Angeles in *Rise of the Labor Movement in Los Angeles* (Berkeley: University of California Press, 1955); Louis B. and Richard S. Perry pick up in 1911 and continue to 1941 in *A History of the Los Angeles Labor Movement* (Los Angeles: Institute of Industrial Relations, University of California, 1963). Robert E. L. Knight recounts the Bay Area history in *Industrial Relations in the San Francisco Bay Area, 1900–1918* (Berkeley: University of California Press, 1960).

These general accounts are surrounded by a sizable—and still growing—literature focused far more tightly on specific unions, industries, periods, areas. Many of these are valuable, especially to the serious reader, but they cannot make up for the lack of a good, broad-gauged general account. If the reader, though, is willing to wade into the deeper waters of these studies, monographs, and dissertations, Mitchell Slobodek provided a highly useful map of the territory in his *A Selective Bibliography of California Labor History* (Los Angeles: Institute of Industrial Relations, University of California, 1964). It needs updating now

but at the time of its publication it provided a highly useful cata-
logue of conveniently classified, annotated citations.

Happily, scholars are becoming more interested in expanding
their focus to bring the workers' response to society and industry into a broader context. Increasingly, they are going beyond
unions and industrial relations, as such, to the quality of the
lives of working people. The development, continued and extended, can add much to labor history in substance and texture
and understanding. By way of example, the works of Alexander
Saxton, *The Indispensable Enemy: Labor and the Anti-Chinese
Movement* (Berkeley: University of California Press, 1971); Neil
Shumsky, "Tar Flat and Nob Hill: A Social History of Industrial
San Francisco during the 1870s" (Ph.D. dissertation, University
of California, Berkeley, 1972); and Jules Tygiel, "Workingmen
in San Francisco, 1880–1901" (Ph.D. dissertation, University
of California, Los Angeles, 1977) add much to the often-told
account of Dennis Kearney and the Workingmen's Party of
California.

A series of booklets, dealing with collective bargaining patterns in specific industries—longshore, agriculture, motion pic-
tures, construction, among others—provides useful close-up
accounts. Published in the mid-1950s by the Institute of Industrial Relations at the University of California, Berkeley, the
series could usefully be updated and its coverage extended.
Countless studies, theses, dissertations, most of them unpub-
lished, throw additional light in these areas.

The story of farm labor in California is thoroughly docu-
mented. Carleton H. Parker's *The Casual Laborer and Other Essays* (New York: Harcourt, Brace and Howe, 1920) provides a
dramatic and revealing introduction. Carey McWilliams's *Factories in the Fields* (Boston: Little Brown, 1939) is indispensable.
(His works on *Southern California Country: An Island on the
Land* [New York: Duell, Sloan & Pearce, 1946] and *California:
The Great Exception* [1949; Santa Barbara: Peregrine Smith,
1976], though far more general, are useful and provocative.)
The several works of Ernesto Galarza are a necessary account
of the bracero period. The rise of the United Farm Workers and
the story of César Chávez, its leader, have been told in a still-
growing list of books. Dick Meister's eyewitness account in *A
Long Time Coming: The Struggle to Unionize Farm Workers,* with

Anne Loftis (New York: MacMillan, 1977) is an important source. So are, in their individual ways, Jacques Levy's *César Chávez: Autobiography of La Causa* (New York: Norton, 1975); *Sal Si Puedes* (New York: Random House, 1969) by Peter Matthiessen; Ronald B. Taylor's *Sweatshops in the Sun* (Boston: Beacon Press, 1973) and *Chavez and the Farm Workers* (Boston: Beacon Press, 1975); and many more. It has been a popular area of study and reportage in recent years.

The U. S. Senate Committee on Education and Labor, known usually as the La Follette Committee (after its chairman, Senator Robert M. La Follette, Jr.), explored many aspects of labor relations that are of immediate concern to the student of California history. Its hearings and reports examined the antiunion and open-shop activities of both Los Angeles and San Francisco employers, the vigorous and sometimes violent response of the Associated Farmers to efforts of farm workers to organize, and more. It utilized cogent background and research reports by Paul Taylor, Clark Kerr, Varden Fuller, and other perceptive students of the California labor scene. They are an essential part of the record of the 1930s. (See various hearings and reports of the U. S. Congress, Senate, Committee on Education and Labor, "Violations of the Right of Free Speech and Assembly...," *Hearings,* 76th, 77th, and 78th Congresses (1940–1944).

Labor relations in the public sector in California are of such relatively recent origin that the scholarly analysis has only begun. The field can hardly be covered, however, without the detailed and enormously useful reportage of the California Public Employee Relations Program at the Institute of Industrial Relations, University of California, Berkeley. More is bound to come. An area even less often tapped is that constantly explored since the mid-1950s by public opinion research. The tapes of the Field Research Corporation, for example, are available through the University of California Data Program at Berkeley. Its samplings of public opinion over a quarter of a century offer vast arrays of information that beg for study and analysis. Its almost continuous use of union members, union families, or working people as discrete groups offer fertile ground for thoughtful examination.

A start has been made on oral histories of working people, union leadership, and active participants in labor relations (arbitrators, mediators, attorneys, and others); their literal testimony can supply substance and, not infrequently, valuable insights. The future of useful, relevant, interesting labor history lies, I think, in this direction. I hope labor historians, and labor as well, will get on with the job.

# INDEX